Building Future-Ready Software

Advanced Cross-Platform Development with Python and C# for a Connected, Digital World

THOMPSON CARTER

Table of Content

TABLE OF CONTENTS

Introduction

Welcome to **"Building Future-Ready Software: Advanced Cross-Platform Development with Python and C# for a Connected, Digital World"**. In today's fast-paced technological landscape, the demand for cross-platform applications has never been higher. Whether it's mobile, desktop, or web, users expect seamless, intuitive experiences across a wide variety of devices and operating systems. Cross-platform development empowers developers to meet this demand by creating applications that work across multiple platforms with a single codebase, significantly reducing development time and effort while expanding their reach.

This book is a comprehensive guide for developers who want to master the art of cross-platform development using **Python** and **C#**. These two programming languages are highly versatile, each with its own strengths in building robust, scalable, and high-performance applications. While Python is celebrated for its simplicity and ease of use, C# brings the power of the **.NET ecosystem**, enabling developers to build powerful cross-platform apps with native performance. By focusing on these two languages, we can unlock the full potential of cross-platform development and enable you to create universal applications that are future-ready.

Throughout this book, we will explore the tools, libraries, frameworks, and best practices necessary to succeed in building cross-platform applications. We will look at how to seamlessly integrate backend services, handle data synchronization, and design rich, responsive user interfaces. You'll gain a solid understanding of cloud integration, real-time data synchronization, and working with APIs. Most importantly, you'll learn how to take advantage of both **Python** and **C#** to create applications that are not only functional but also optimized for performance and scalability across all platforms.

Who This Book Is For

This book is intended for intermediate to advanced developers who are familiar with basic programming concepts and are looking to expand their knowledge of cross-platform development. If you have prior experience with either **Python** or **C#** and want to build powerful applications that can run across multiple platforms— whether mobile, desktop, or web—this book will provide you with the tools and techniques you need to succeed.

If you're new to cross-platform development but have experience with either Python or C#, you'll find this book to be a practical, step-by-step guide to building real-world applications. If you're already proficient in cross-platform development, this book will introduce you to new libraries, tools, and advanced techniques that will help you take your skills to the next level.

What You'll Learn

In this book, we will guide you through the process of building and deploying cross-platform applications from start to finish, focusing on Python and C# as the core languages for development. You will learn how to:

1. **Get Started with Cross-Platform Development**: Understand the fundamentals of cross-platform development, including the principles behind building universal applications that work seamlessly across different platforms.

2. **Master the Tools and Frameworks**: Dive deep into popular cross-platform frameworks like **React Native**, **Xamarin**, **Flutter**, and **Kivy**, and learn how to leverage the power of each for creating modern, high-performance applications.

3. **Develop Cross-Platform UIs**: Learn how to design user interfaces that are optimized for different screen sizes, resolutions, and interaction models. You'll explore how to use responsive design and platform-specific UI conventions to create polished, consistent experiences across platforms.

4. **Integrate Cloud Services and Backend**: Discover how to integrate cloud-based services such as **Firebase**, **AWS**, and **Google Cloud** for authentication, real-time data synchronization, and storage. You'll learn how to manage backend integration seamlessly and handle complex data operations.

5. **Optimize Performance**: Get hands-on tips and techniques for optimizing the performance of your applications, from managing memory and CPU usage to optimizing startup times and UI rendering. You'll learn how to ensure that your apps run smoothly on a variety of devices, including mobile and desktop.

6. **Test, Debug, and Deploy Your App**: Explore best practices for testing cross-platform applications,

including unit testing, integration testing, and debugging across different platforms. You'll also learn how to deploy your app to the **Google Play Store**, **Apple App Store**, and cloud services, while automating your deployment pipeline using CI/CD tools.

Why Cross-Platform Development Matters

Cross-platform development is more important than ever as the demand for applications that work across multiple platforms continues to grow. In the past, developers had to write separate code for each platform, whether it was iOS, Android, or desktop. This was time-consuming, costly, and error-prone. With cross-platform frameworks, developers can write a single codebase that runs across different platforms, saving time and resources while still delivering native-like performance.

The shift towards **cross-platform development** is also driven by the rise of mobile devices, IoT, and the increasing importance of cloud services. As users expect applications to be available on multiple devices and platforms, developers must be able to deliver a consistent experience across all of them. This book will equip you with the knowledge and tools to meet these challenges head-on and build future-ready applications that can scale, perform well, and adapt to a constantly evolving digital world.

The Road Ahead

By the end of this book, you will have gained in-depth knowledge of the cross-platform development landscape, a clear understanding of the tools and frameworks at your disposal, and the skills necessary to start building your own cross-platform applications. You'll be able to integrate cutting-edge technologies like **AI**, **machine learning**, **IoT**, and **cloud services** into your applications, ensuring that they remain at the forefront of innovation.

The journey you're about to undertake will transform the way you approach software development. You'll learn how to write applications that work seamlessly on all devices and platforms, providing users with a consistent, intuitive experience wherever they are. Whether you're creating an app for the mobile market, building a desktop application, or launching a web app, this book will serve as your guide to mastering cross-platform development.

We hope this book will inspire you to take the next step in your development career and start building the next generation of cross-platform applications. Let's dive in!

CHAPTER 1

INTRODUCTION TO CROSS-PLATFORM DEVELOPMENT

Overview of Cross-Platform Development and Its Growing Importance in the Digital World

Cross-platform development refers to the practice of building software that can run on multiple platforms, such as Windows, macOS, Linux, iOS, and Android, without requiring significant changes to the codebase. The goal is to write one set of code that works seamlessly across different environments, saving time and resources in the development process.

In today's interconnected world, the demand for applications that work consistently across a variety of devices is higher than ever. With the proliferation of mobile devices, smart TVs, tablets, and wearables, businesses must deliver their products on all platforms to stay competitive. Whether you are developing a mobile app, web application, or desktop program, being able to run your software on multiple devices is crucial.

Historically, developers had to create separate applications for each platform, resulting in lengthy development cycles, increased costs, and more complex maintenance. However, advancements in cross-platform development have changed this landscape, enabling developers to build applications that work across multiple operating systems and devices.

Why Python and C# Are Great Choices for Building Scalable, Versatile Software

Both Python and C# are powerful programming languages that are highly suited for cross-platform development. Here's why:

1. **Python**:

- o **Versatility**: Python is known for its simplicity and readability, making it an ideal choice for both beginners and experienced developers. It is used in web development, data science, machine learning, automation, and more. Libraries such as Kivy, BeeWare, and PyQt allow developers to build cross-platform applications efficiently.

- o **Community and Libraries**: Python has a massive community and a wealth of open-source libraries, making it easier to find solutions to common problems. With frameworks like Django and Flask for web development and Kivy for mobile apps, Python offers flexible options for different types of projects.

- o **Portability**: Python runs on all major platforms, including Windows, macOS, and Linux. This cross-platform compatibility allows developers to write code once and deploy it anywhere, reducing the time and effort needed for platform-specific changes.

18

2. **C#:**

- **Strong Support for Cross-Platform Development**: C# was originally designed for Windows applications but has evolved to be a powerful tool for cross-platform development, especially with the advent of .NET Core (now .NET 5+). .NET Core allows C# developers to build applications for macOS, Linux, and mobile devices.

- **Xamarin for Mobile Apps**: Xamarin is a powerful cross-platform framework that allows developers to build native mobile apps for both Android and iOS using C#. With Xamarin, you can share the majority of the code between the two platforms, making development faster and more efficient.

- **Mature Ecosystem**: C# benefits from a rich set of tools and libraries, particularly within the Microsoft ecosystem. With features like Visual Studio, powerful debugging, and cloud integration, C# remains a top choice for enterprise-level applications.

Together, Python and C# offer a diverse range of capabilities, whether you're building a mobile app, web service, or desktop application.

Key Trends in Software Development, Including the Shift Toward Cross-Platform Solutions

As the tech industry rapidly evolves, several key trends are shaping the future of software development:

1. **Increased Demand for Multi-Platform Solutions**: The growing use of smartphones, tablets, wearables, and smart home devices means that applications must work across all these platforms. Developers can no longer afford to focus on one specific platform but must build software that reaches users wherever they are, whether on iOS, Android, or the web.

2. **Agile and DevOps Practices**: Agile development and DevOps practices are becoming more popular, focusing on delivering software faster and more efficiently. Cross-platform development aligns well with these practices by allowing faster iteration cycles and simplified deployment strategies.

3. **Cloud Computing and Integration**: Cloud-based solutions are becoming increasingly popular, providing scalability, security, and flexibility. With cross-platform development, integrating cloud services (such as APIs, storage, and databases) into apps becomes simpler, offering a unified experience for users across platforms.

4. **Rise of Progressive Web Apps (PWAs)**: PWAs are web apps that function similarly to native apps, providing offline support and push notifications. PWAs are gaining traction as they work across multiple devices and can be deployed with minimal

effort. This highlights the need for cross-platform capabilities in modern app development.

Real-World Example: A Company Building a Mobile App Using Both Python and C#

Imagine a company developing a fitness tracking mobile app. The goal is to create an app that works on both Android and iOS, with a backend that can handle user data securely.

- **Using Python**: The company uses Python for the backend API, utilizing frameworks like Flask or FastAPI to create a RESTful service that interacts with the database, stores user data, and handles authentication.
- **Using C#**: For the mobile app, they use Xamarin to write the frontend in C#. This allows the company to write the majority of the code once and deploy it to both Android and iOS. Xamarin provides access to native APIs, ensuring the app looks and feels like a native app on both platforms.

By combining Python for the backend and C# for the frontend, the company reduces the amount of duplicated code, shortens development time, and ensures a consistent experience across platforms. The app can be easily updated, and since both Python and C# are mature, the development team can leverage vast libraries, community support, and best practices to build a scalable and high-performance app.

In this chapter, we've introduced the fundamental concepts behind cross-platform development and explained why Python and C# are excellent choices for building future-ready software. The growing importance of multi-platform solutions is evident, as businesses must deliver software that meets the needs of an increasingly diverse set of devices. In the next chapters, we'll dive deeper into the tools and techniques used to develop cross-platform applications with Python and C#.

CHAPTER 2

THE EVOLUTION OF SOFTWARE DEVELOPMENT

A Brief History of Software Development: From Monolithic Applications to Microservices and Cloud-Native Solutions

The landscape of software development has evolved dramatically over the past few decades, shaped by technological advances, shifting user needs, and the push for more flexible and scalable solutions. Here's a quick overview of this transformation:

1. **Monolithic Applications**:

    o **Early Days**: In the early days of software development, most applications were monolithic. This means they were built as a single, unified unit. All the components—user interface, logic, and data access—were tightly coupled into one large codebase.

24

o **Challenges**: While monolithic applications worked well for small projects, they became difficult to scale, maintain, and update as they grew. Making changes to one part of the application often required rebuilding and redeploying the entire system, which led to longer development cycles and more risk of introducing bugs.

o **Example**: A traditional enterprise application for managing customer data, where the backend, frontend, and database were all integrated into a single codebase.

2. **The Shift to Microservices**:

o **Emergence**: As systems became more complex, the monolithic approach gave way to microservices architecture. Microservices break applications into smaller, independent services that can communicate with each other through APIs. Each microservice is designed to perform a specific task (such as user authentication or processing payments), making the system more modular and easier to scale.

- o **Advantages**: Microservices allow for continuous integration and deployment (CI/CD), faster updates, and better fault tolerance. Each service can be developed, tested, and deployed independently, reducing the risk of breaking the whole system when changes are made.

- o **Example**: A modern e-commerce platform might break down the checkout, user profile, and inventory services into separate microservices that can be scaled independently as the demand for each feature fluctuates.

3. **Cloud-Native Solutions**:

- o **Cloud Adoption**: The advent of cloud computing revolutionized how software is developed, deployed, and maintained. Cloud-native development focuses on building applications that are designed to run in the cloud environment. These applications are typically built using microservices and are scalable, resilient, and easy to maintain.

- o **Key Concepts**: Cloud-native solutions leverage containers (such as Docker), orchestration tools (such as Kubernetes), and serverless computing to ensure that applications can scale and operate efficiently in a distributed, cloud-based environment.

- o **Example**: A cloud-native application could be an IoT platform that connects devices, collects data, and analyzes it in real time, all while utilizing the elasticity of cloud computing to handle fluctuating workloads.

Introduction to Cross-Platform Tools and Frameworks

With the rise of cloud-native and microservices architectures, the need for cross-platform tools has grown, enabling developers to write applications that work seamlessly across multiple devices, platforms, and operating systems. Cross-platform development frameworks allow software to run on various platforms without needing to rewrite the codebase for each one.

Here are some of the most widely-used cross-platform tools and frameworks:

1. **React Native**:
   - A popular framework for building mobile applications using JavaScript and React. It allows developers to write code once and deploy it to both iOS and Android devices, ensuring that the app has a native look and feel on both platforms.

2. **Xamarin**:
   - A Microsoft-backed framework that allows developers to build native apps for iOS, Android, and Windows using C#. Xamarin provides access to platform-specific APIs, so you can create fully native apps while sharing a large portion of the code across platforms.

3. **Flutter**:

   o A relatively new but rapidly growing framework developed by Google. Flutter uses the Dart programming language to build high-performance, natively compiled applications for mobile, web, and desktop from a single codebase.

4. **Electron**:

   o For desktop applications, Electron allows you to use web technologies (HTML, CSS, and JavaScript) to build cross-platform desktop apps. Popular apps like Visual Studio Code and Slack are built using Electron.

5. **Kivy**:

   o A Python framework for building multi-touch applications, particularly suited for mobile apps. Kivy allows developers to build cross-platform apps that can run on Android, iOS, Linux, macOS, and Windows.

These frameworks provide a unified solution to the problem of developing software for different platforms, allowing developers to focus on writing the logic and functionality rather than worrying about the specifics of each platform.

Real-World Example: How a Startup Transitioned from a Single-Platform App to a Multi-Platform Solution

Let's consider a real-world scenario of a startup that initially developed a mobile app for iOS only. The app is a fitness tracker, providing users with the ability to log their workouts, track their progress, and share their achievements with others. While the app had a solid user base, the startup began receiving feedback from users who wanted to access the app on Android devices as well.

Initially, the company considered building a separate Android version of the app. However, this would require hiring additional developers and duplicating much of the work. Instead, they decided to adopt a cross-platform approach.

Here's how they made the transition:

1. **Choosing Xamarin**: After evaluating several frameworks, the team decided to use Xamarin. They chose Xamarin because they were already using C# for the iOS app, and Xamarin would allow them to reuse a significant portion of their code while developing a fully native Android app.

2. **Development Process**: The team started by building the Android version using Xamarin, reusing most of the logic from the iOS app. They had to make some adjustments for platform-specific features, such as Android's back button and material design, but the majority of the user interface code was shared between both platforms.

3. **Deployment**: After developing the Android app, the team tested it across both platforms to ensure that the user experience was consistent. Once they were satisfied with the results, they deployed both the iOS and Android apps simultaneously, significantly reducing the time-to-market for the new version.

4. **Results**: By adopting a cross-platform solution with Xamarin, the startup not only saved time and resources but also created a consistent user experience across both iOS and Android. They were able to expand their customer base and increase user engagement by reaching a broader audience.

In this case, the startup's decision to transition to a cross-platform approach allowed them to scale their application more efficiently while maintaining the quality and consistency of their product. This shift highlights how adopting the right cross-platform tools can empower developers to grow their apps across multiple platforms without starting from scratch.

This chapter provides a historical overview of software development, tracing its evolution from monolithic to microservices and cloud-native architectures. It also introduces key cross-platform tools and frameworks that help developers deliver multi-platform solutions. In the next chapter, we will delve deeper into Python and C#, exploring why they are ideal choices for building future-ready software.

CHAPTER 3

PYTHON FOR CROSS-PLATFORM DEVELOPMENT

Exploring Python's Role in Modern Software Engineering

Python has become one of the most popular and versatile programming languages in modern software engineering. Known for its simplicity and readability, Python enables developers to build a wide range of applications, from simple scripts to complex, enterprise-grade systems. One of its most significant advantages is its ability to work seamlessly across different platforms, making it a prime choice for cross-platform development.

Here are some reasons why Python plays such a pivotal role in modern software engineering:

1. **Ease of Learning and Use**:

- o Python is often regarded as one of the easiest programming languages to learn due to its clean syntax. Its simplicity allows developers to focus on solving problems rather than getting bogged down by complex syntax rules.

- o This makes Python an attractive option for both beginners and experienced developers, and it's widely used in both educational environments and professional settings.

2. **Cross-Platform Compatibility**:

- o Python's compatibility across all major operating systems—Windows, macOS, and Linux—makes it ideal for cross-platform development. Python's "write once, run anywhere" philosophy means that developers can write code on one platform and expect it to run seamlessly on others.

- o Python achieves this by abstracting away the underlying OS-specific details, allowing developers to focus on writing application logic instead of dealing with system-specific configurations.

3. **Strong Community and Open-Source Libraries**:

   o Python has a massive and active community that contributes to a rich ecosystem of libraries and frameworks. This community-driven development accelerates problem-solving by providing tools and resources that allow developers to implement common tasks without reinventing the wheel.

4. **Flexibility Across Domains**:

   o Python's versatility means it can be used across various domains, from web development (with Django and Flask) to data science (with Pandas, NumPy, and SciPy), automation (with Selenium and PyAutoGUI), and even game development (with Pygame). This makes Python a great choice for building cross-platform applications in diverse fields.

Key Python Libraries and Frameworks Used in Cross-Platform Development

Python's power in cross-platform development is significantly amplified by the many libraries and frameworks available. These tools help streamline the development process, enabling developers to build applications that run seamlessly on different platforms. Here are some key Python libraries and frameworks that are widely used for cross-platform development:

1. **Kivy**:

   o Kivy is an open-source Python library for developing multi-touch applications. It's particularly useful for mobile applications but can also be used for desktop applications. Kivy provides support for gestures, touch input, and other features that are essential for mobile platforms.

37

- o It allows developers to write cross-platform apps that work on Android, iOS, Linux, macOS, and Windows with minimal code changes.

2. **BeeWare**:

- o BeeWare is a collection of tools and libraries for building native user interfaces using Python. It allows developers to write applications that run on multiple platforms, including Windows, macOS, Linux, iOS, and Android.

- o BeeWare provides tools like Toga (a GUI framework) and Briefcase (a tool for packaging Python applications into standalone apps) to make cross-platform development smoother and more accessible.

3. **PyQt/PySide**:

- o PyQt and PySide are set of Python bindings for the Qt application framework. Qt is a powerful, cross-platform GUI toolkit that allows developers to create rich graphical user interfaces for their applications.

o These libraries provide the tools needed to build high-quality desktop applications that run on multiple operating systems, including Windows, macOS, and Linux.

4. **Flask/Django**:

   o While Flask and Django are web frameworks, they are still essential when it comes to building cross-platform web applications. Python web frameworks like Flask (a lightweight framework) and Django (a more full-featured framework) allow developers to create dynamic web applications that work across any platform with a browser.

   o These frameworks are both scalable and flexible, making them perfect for web applications that need to be accessible on any device, from desktops to mobile phones.

5. **PyInstaller**:

   o PyInstaller is a Python library that helps convert Python programs into standalone executable files.

This is especially useful for cross-platform development because it allows you to package a Python application into a binary that can be run independently of the Python interpreter.

- ○ PyInstaller supports a variety of platforms, including Windows, macOS, and Linux, and simplifies the distribution of Python applications across different environments.

6. **Tkinter**:

- ○ Tkinter is the standard GUI toolkit that comes bundled with Python. It provides a simple way to build desktop applications with graphical interfaces. Though not as feature-rich as PyQt or Kivy, Tkinter is an easy way to build basic cross-platform applications that can run on Windows, macOS, and Linux.

Real-World Example: Building a Simple Python App That Runs Across Multiple Platforms

Let's walk through a real-world example of how a simple Python app can be developed and deployed across multiple platforms using Kivy.

Scenario: A developer is tasked with building a basic "To-Do List" app that allows users to add tasks, mark them as completed, and delete tasks. The app should run on Android, iOS, Windows, and macOS.

1. **Setting Up the Environment**:

   o The developer starts by installing Kivy on their development machine. Kivy provides detailed instructions for setting up the development environment on Windows, macOS, and Linux.

   o They also install additional tools like Buildozer (for building Android apps) and Xcode (for building iOS apps).

2. **Writing the Code**:

   o The developer writes the core application logic using Python and Kivy. Here's a simplified version of the code:

```python
Copy
from kivy.app import App
from kivy.uix.button import Button
from kivy.uix.textinput import TextInput
from kivy.uix.boxlayout import BoxLayout

class ToDoApp(App):
    def build(self):
        self.layout                          =
BoxLayout(orientation='vertical')
        self.task_input                      =
TextInput(hint_text="Enter a task")
        self.add_button = Button(text="Add
Task")
```

```
self.add_button.bind(on_press=self.add_ta
sk)

self.layout.add_widget(self.task_input)

self.layout.add_widget(self.add_button)
        return self.layout

    def add_task(self, instance):
        task = self.task_input.text
        print(f"Task added: {task}")
        self.task_input.text = ""  # Clear
input field

if __name__ == '__main__':
    ToDoApp().run()
```

This basic app allows users to input tasks, and when
the "Add Task" button is pressed, the task is added
to the console.

3. **Running the App Locally**:

   o The developer tests the app on their local machine (Windows or macOS) by simply running the Python script. Since Kivy is cross-platform, the app runs seamlessly without needing any changes.

4. **Packaging for Mobile**:

   o To deploy the app on Android and iOS, the developer uses Buildozer (for Android) and Xcode (for iOS). Buildozer compiles the Python app into an APK file that can be installed on Android devices, while Xcode allows packaging it for iOS.

5. **Deploying the App**:

   o After testing the app on each platform, the developer can distribute it via the Google Play Store or Apple App Store for mobile users, or package it as an executable for desktop users.

In this example, Kivy allowed the developer to write the core application code once and deploy it across multiple platforms with minimal effort. The use of Python and Kivy ensured that the application was both cross-platform and easy to maintain.

This chapter has explored Python's pivotal role in modern software engineering, particularly its strengths in cross-platform development. By leveraging the power of Python's libraries and frameworks, developers can create software that runs seamlessly across different platforms. In the next chapter, we'll look at C# and its powerful capabilities for cross-platform development.

CHAPTER 4

C# FOR CROSS-PLATFORM DEVELOPMENT

Introduction to C# and Its Capabilities for Cross-Platform

Applications

C# is a modern, object-oriented programming language developed by Microsoft, known for its versatility and robustness in building various types of applications, from web and mobile to desktop and game development. Initially, C# was designed for developing Windows-based applications, but with the rise of .NET Core (now just .NET), C# has expanded its reach, enabling developers to build applications that run on multiple platforms, including Windows, macOS, and Linux.

Here's why C# is an excellent choice for cross-platform development:

1. **Cross-Platform Development with .NET Core**:

   o .NET Core, the open-source, cross-platform version of the .NET framework, enables C# to be used for building applications that run on different operating systems. With the transition to .NET 5 and later versions, C# has become a powerful tool for developing web apps, APIs, and mobile apps that work seamlessly across platforms.

   o C# on .NET Core allows developers to write applications that are fully platform-agnostic, giving them the flexibility to target Windows, macOS, and Linux without needing to worry about platform-specific code.

2. **Unified Development Environment**:

   o Unlike earlier versions of .NET, which were primarily Windows-centric, .NET Core has unified the development environment. Developers can now use Visual Studio Code (VS

47

Code) or Visual Studio across platforms, making development more streamlined and efficient.

- o .NET 6 (and later versions) continue to build upon the cross-platform nature, providing a consistent development experience whether you're working on a Windows, macOS, or Linux machine.

3. **Rich Ecosystem and Tools**:

- o C# is supported by a vast ecosystem of libraries and frameworks that make it an ideal choice for modern application development. From web development with ASP.NET Core to mobile development with Xamarin, the C# ecosystem provides developers with powerful tools to build high-quality, scalable cross-platform apps.

Tools and Libraries in C# for Developing Cross-Platform Apps

There are several tools and libraries in the C# ecosystem that facilitate cross-platform development. Here are some of the most important ones:

1. **Xamarin**:

   o Xamarin is a Microsoft-backed framework that allows developers to write native mobile applications for iOS and Android using C#. With Xamarin, you can write a single codebase for both platforms and access platform-specific APIs when needed.

   o Xamarin makes use of the Mono runtime to enable cross-platform development, and it allows sharing code between Android, iOS, and even Windows. Xamarin Forms, a part of Xamarin, provides a way to create UIs that work across both Android and iOS.

2. **.NET MAUI (Multi-platform App UI)**:

o .NET MAUI is the next-generation framework for building cross-platform mobile and desktop apps using C#. It is the successor to Xamarin.Forms and supports building apps for iOS, Android, macOS, and Windows from a single codebase.

o .NET MAUI simplifies development by providing a unified UI toolkit, which means developers can create applications that share UI elements and logic across platforms, significantly reducing development time.

3. **Blazor**:

o Blazor is a framework within .NET for building interactive web applications using C# instead of JavaScript. It allows developers to write client-side web applications with C#, running in the browser via WebAssembly or on the server using SignalR for real-time communication.

o   Blazor enables developers to share code between the server and the client, creating a more unified development experience for web applications.

4. **ASP.NET Core**:

o   ASP.NET Core is a high-performance, open-source web framework built on .NET Core. It is widely used for building cross-platform web applications, APIs, and microservices. ASP.NET Core works on Windows, Linux, and macOS, offering a powerful solution for server-side development.

o   It integrates with a variety of other libraries and tools for building full-stack applications, making it ideal for developing scalable, cross-platform web services.

5. **Unity**:

o   Although Unity is a game development engine, it uses C# as its primary scripting language, making it possible to develop cross-platform games for

PC, consoles, mobile devices, and even VR/AR platforms.

- o Unity's cross-platform capabilities and wide support for various platforms (e.g., iOS, Android, PlayStation, Xbox, and WebGL) make it a powerful tool for game developers who want to reach a broad audience.

6. **Avalonia**:

- o Avalonia is a cross-platform UI framework for .NET, similar to WPF (Windows Presentation Foundation). It allows developers to create desktop applications with rich UIs that run on Windows, Linux, and macOS.
- o Avalonia provides a high-performance solution for developers who want to create native desktop applications across multiple platforms without relying on platform-specific tools.

Real-World Example: Developing a Desktop Application Using C#

and .NET Core

Let's consider a real-world example of developing a desktop application for managing personal finances using C# and .NET Core. The application needs to run on Windows, macOS, and Linux, providing users with the ability to track their income and expenses, generate reports, and visualize financial trends.

1. **Choosing .NET Core for Cross-Platform Compatibility**:

    o The developer decides to use .NET Core for this project due to its ability to run on multiple operating systems and its excellent performance. Since the goal is to build a cross-platform desktop app, they choose to use **Avalonia** as the UI framework, as it supports Windows, macOS, and Linux.

2. **Setting Up the Project**:

o The developer sets up a new **.NET Core** project using Visual Studio Code, which is cross-platform and works on Windows, macOS, and Linux. They install the **Avalonia** template to build the GUI, ensuring that the app will work seamlessly on all platforms.

3. **Designing the User Interface**:

o Using Avalonia's XAML-based layout system, the developer creates a modern, user-friendly interface for the finance tracker. The app includes text fields for entering income and expenses, buttons for adding new entries, and a chart to visualize financial data.

o The UI components are designed to look and behave the same on all three platforms, leveraging Avalonia's cross-platform capabilities.

4. **Writing the Core Application Logic**:

o The developer writes the core logic for tracking income and expenses, storing data in an SQLite database, and calculating balances. They also implement features like sorting, filtering, and generating financial reports.

o   This logic is written once in C#, and since the backend doesn't depend on platform-specific libraries, it works seamlessly across Windows, macOS, and Linux.

5. **Testing the Application**:

o   The developer tests the app on all three platforms by running the application locally. Thanks to .NET Core and Avalonia, the app behaves consistently on each platform, and no platform-specific issues arise during testing.

6. **Packaging and Deployment**:

o   The developer uses the **.NET Core CLI** (Command-Line Interface) to package the application for distribution. They create platform-specific executables for Windows, macOS, and Linux using the .NET Core publish commands.

55

o The app is packaged and ready for distribution via platforms like GitHub or a custom website, with all users receiving the same high-quality experience regardless of their operating system.

This example demonstrates how C# and .NET Core enable the development of cross-platform desktop applications with minimal overhead. By leveraging frameworks like Avalonia, developers can focus on creating robust functionality and engaging UIs, while ensuring the application runs smoothly across multiple platforms.

In this chapter, we've explored C#'s potential for cross-platform development and discussed key tools and frameworks like Xamarin, .NET MAUI, Blazor, and Avalonia. These tools make C# a powerful language for building applications that span multiple platforms. In the next chapter, we'll dive into the role of APIs in cross-platform development and how to integrate them into your

projects.

CHAPTER 5

SETTING UP YOUR DEVELOPMENT ENVIRONMENT

Installing and Setting Up Python and C# Development Environments

Setting up a proper development environment is the first crucial step in ensuring an efficient and smooth development process, especially when working on cross-platform projects that involve multiple programming languages like Python and C#. Both Python and C# have specific setups that need to be configured, but once properly set up, they provide a robust and scalable environment for development.

Here's how you can get started with the Python and C# development environments:

1. Setting Up Python

To begin using Python for cross-platform development, you need to install the Python interpreter and any necessary libraries or frameworks that you will use. Here's how you can get started:

- **Step 1: Install Python**:
    - o **Windows**: Download the latest version of Python from the official Python website (https://www.python.org/downloads/). During installation, make sure to check the box to add Python to your system's PATH.
    - o **macOS**: Python is pre-installed on macOS, but it's often a good idea to install the latest version using Homebrew by running `brew install python`.
    - o **Linux**: Most Linux distributions come with Python pre-installed. However, you can install the latest version by running `sudo apt install python3` on Ubuntu-based systems.
- **Step 2: Install Package Manager (pip)**:

o Python uses `pip` as its package manager to install third-party libraries. It is usually installed by default. You can verify if `pip` is installed by running `pip --version` in your terminal.

o Install libraries by running `pip install <library_name>`. For example, to install Kivy for cross-platform development, you would run `pip install kivy`.

- **Step 3: Install Cross-Platform Frameworks**:

    o If you plan to use frameworks like **Kivy**, **BeeWare**, or **Flask/Django**, you'll need to install them using `pip`. For example, to install Kivy, run `pip install kivy`.

2. Setting Up C#

To set up a C# development environment, you will need to install .NET and an IDE. Here's the setup process:

- **Step 1: Install .NET SDK**:

- **Windows/Mac/Linux**: The .NET SDK provides all the tools you need to build .NET applications, including C#. Download the SDK from the official .NET website (https://dotnet.microsoft.com/download).

- After installation, verify that .NET is installed by running the command `dotnet --version` in your terminal or command prompt.

- **Step 2: Install Visual Studio**:

  - For a full-featured C# development environment, Microsoft's **Visual Studio** is an excellent choice. Visual Studio offers support for building web, desktop, mobile, and cloud applications.

  - **Windows**: Download Visual Studio from the official website (https://visualstudio.microsoft.com/) and select the C# development workload during installation.

  - **macOS**: You can also install **Visual Studio for Mac** (https://visualstudio.microsoft.com/vs/mac/), which provides a similar experience as Visual Studio on Windows.

- **Step 3: Install Xamarin/MAUI (Optional)**:

  o For mobile development, install Xamarin or **.NET MAUI** (Multi-platform App UI) to build cross-platform apps. Both Xamarin and .NET MAUI allow you to write applications that run on Android, iOS, macOS, and Windows using a single C# codebase.

  o You can install Xamarin through Visual Studio's installer by selecting the **Mobile development with .NET** workload.

Cross-Platform IDEs and Tools

When working on cross-platform projects that involve multiple programming languages, choosing the right Integrated Development Environment (IDE) or code editor is critical. Here are some of the best cross-platform tools for Python and C# development:

1. Visual Studio Code (VS Code)

Visual Studio Code is a popular open-source code editor developed by Microsoft. It is lightweight, highly customizable, and supports a wide range of programming languages, including Python and C#. VS Code works on Windows, macOS, and Linux and is ideal for cross-platform development.

- **Features**:
    o Cross-platform compatibility.

    o Integrated terminal for running commands and tests.

    o Wide range of extensions for Python, C#, Git, Docker, and more.

    o Excellent support for debugging, IntelliSense (code completion), and version control.

- **Installation**:
    o Download and install VS Code from https://code.visualstudio.com/.

- Install the **Python** extension and **C#** extension (C# support is provided through the **C# for Visual Studio Code (powered by OmniSharp)** extension).

- VS Code provides all the necessary tools and extensions to work with both Python and C# within the same IDE.

2. JetBrains Rider

JetBrains Rider is a powerful, full-featured IDE for .NET development, including C#. Rider offers advanced code analysis, debugging, and seamless integration with .NET Core, Xamarin, and .NET MAUI for cross-platform development.

- **Features**:

  - Full support for .NET, Xamarin, .NET Core, and MAUI.

- Cross-platform support (Windows, macOS, Linux).

- Advanced debugging and refactoring tools.

- Smart code completion and analysis for both Python (via a plugin) and C#.

- **Installation**:

  - Rider can be downloaded from https://www.jetbrains.com/rider/.

  - It comes with integrated support for both C# and Python (via plugins), making it a great tool for developers working with both languages.

3. Other Tools for Cross-Platform Development

- **Docker**: For containerization and consistent development environments across platforms.

- **Git**: For version control, helping you manage changes across different environments and platforms.

- **Vagrant**: For managing virtual machines and creating cross-platform development environments.

Real-World Example: Setting Up an Integrated Development

Environment for a Project That Uses Both Python and C#

Let's walk through the setup of an integrated development environment for a project that uses both **Python** and **C#**. In this scenario, you are developing a cross-platform application where the backend is built in Python, and the frontend (desktop application) is developed in C# using .NET Core and Avalonia.

Step 1: Installing Visual Studio Code (VS Code)

- Download and install **Visual Studio Code** from https://code.visualstudio.com.

- Install the **Python** and **C#** extensions from the VS Code marketplace.

- Ensure that you have the **.NET SDK** and **Python** installed on your machine.

Step 2: Setting Up Python Backend

- Create a new folder for your project and open it in **VS Code**.

- Open the terminal in VS Code and create a virtual environment for Python:

```bash
Copy
python -m venv env
```

- Activate the virtual environment:

    o **On Windows:** `env\Scripts\activate`

    o **On**   **macOS/Linux:**   `source env/bin/activate`

- Install the necessary Python libraries:

```bash
Copy
pip install flask kivy
```

Step 3: Setting Up C# Frontend (Using .NET Core and Avalonia)

- In the same project folder, create a new C# console application using the **.NET CLI**:

```bash
Copy
dotnet new console -n MyAppFrontend
```

- Open the newly created folder in VS Code and install **Avalonia**:

```bash
Copy
dotnet add package Avalonia
```

- Create the user interface with Avalonia for your desktop application, making sure it will run on Windows, macOS, and Linux.

Step 4: Running and Debugging the Project

- Use the integrated terminal in **VS Code** to run the Python backend with `python app.py`.

68

- Launch the C# Avalonia desktop application using the `.NET CLI` command:

```bash
Copy
dotnet run
```

- Both parts of the application (Python and C#) will run in parallel, and VS Code will provide integrated debugging support for both languages.

In this chapter, we covered the process of setting up the development environment for both Python and C#. We also discussed how cross-platform IDEs like Visual Studio Code and JetBrains Rider help streamline the process when working with multiple languages. In the next chapter, we'll explore the key principles of cross-platform development and best practices for writing cross-platform code.

CHAPTER 6

KEY PRINCIPLES OF CROSS-PLATFORM DEVELOPMENT

Understanding Platform Compatibility, Device Types, and User Experience Considerations

In cross-platform development, it's crucial to design software that works seamlessly across a range of platforms, such as desktops, tablets, and mobile devices. However, while cross-platform development simplifies the process by using a shared codebase, understanding platform compatibility, device types, and user experience (UX) considerations is essential to building effective, high-performing applications.

1. Platform Compatibility

- **Operating Systems**: Platforms include different operating systems, each with unique behaviors, system resources, and restrictions. For example, Windows and macOS have distinct file management systems, user interface conventions, and native libraries. Cross-platform developers need to account for these differences to ensure their apps function properly across environments.

- o **Windows**: Works well with desktop apps, robust support for native applications and desktop APIs.

- o **macOS**: Has unique hardware specifications and strict app guidelines, especially in App Store submissions.

- o **Linux**: Open-source and flexible, but might require additional attention to dependencies and library compatibility.

- **Web vs. Native**: Web applications (running in browsers) are inherently cross-platform, whereas native applications (built for specific platforms like iOS or Android) require more consideration for compatibility.

- o Web apps often face challenges related to browser support, screen sizes, and varying internet speeds.

- o Native apps are built with platform-specific tools and can take advantage of unique hardware features.

- **Device Types**: Device characteristics such as screen size, resolution, and input methods (touch, keyboard, mouse) should be considered to ensure the app's functionality and layout adapt to each platform.

  - o **Mobile devices**: Touch interfaces, small screens, and varying hardware specs.

  - o **Tablets**: Larger touch screens than smartphones, but still have portability concerns.

  - o **Desktops**: Larger screens, keyboard and mouse input, and potentially more powerful hardware.

2. User Experience (UX) Considerations

- **Consistency**: While you want the app to have a consistent look and feel across devices, it's essential to understand that users expect different experiences on different platforms. For example, mobile users expect apps that are optimized for touch interactions, whereas desktop users may be accustomed to keyboard and mouse controls.

- **Responsive Design**: For web and mobile apps, responsive design is key to ensuring that the application adjusts its layout, content, and interactions based on the device's screen size. Tools like CSS media queries and frameworks like Bootstrap or Material UI help create designs that automatically adapt to different screen sizes.

- **Performance**: Mobile devices, especially older models, may have limited processing power, so it's essential to optimize the app's performance. For desktops, you may have more leeway, but it's still important to ensure that your app runs smoothly across different machine specifications.

- **Native Look and Feel**: For mobile or desktop apps, adopting platform-specific design guidelines (e.g.,

Material Design for Android, Human Interface Guidelines for iOS) ensures that the app feels like a native part of the operating system rather than a third-party, cross-platform solution.

Best Practices for Writing Cross-Platform Code

Writing efficient, maintainable, and scalable cross-platform code requires adherence to several best practices. These practices help ensure that the application performs well, minimizes platform-specific code, and provides a consistent experience across devices.

1. Use Cross-Platform Frameworks and Libraries

- Frameworks like **React Native**, **Flutter**, **Xamarin**, and **Kivy** allow developers to write a single codebase and deploy it on multiple platforms. They abstract many platform-specific differences and let you focus on the app's functionality and logic.

74

- For web development, **responsive frameworks** like **Bootstrap** and **Foundation** ensure your app adapts to varying screen sizes.

- **Progressive Web Apps (PWAs)** can also be considered, as they work across devices with web browsers while offering some features of native apps (e.g., offline support, push notifications).

2. Separation of Concerns

- Structure your application so that platform-specific code is isolated from the business logic. This is particularly important for native apps where platform-specific APIs are used. Use an abstraction layer to ensure that platform-dependent code does not interfere with core functionality.

  - For example, in mobile apps, platform-specific UI components or gestures should be abstracted into separate modules that don't affect the rest of the application logic.

3. Optimize for Different Screen Sizes and Resolutions

- Use responsive layouts, scalable vector graphics (SVGs), and flexible UI elements. This allows the app to adapt to different screen sizes and resolutions without losing quality or usability.

- For example, using relative units like percentages and viewport units for layout, instead of fixed pixel sizes, ensures that content scales appropriately on various screen sizes.

4. Consistent and Modular Codebase

- Write clean, modular code that can be reused across platforms. Keeping your codebase organized and modular helps in managing cross-platform functionality. This will also make it easier to update or add new features without breaking compatibility.

- A modular code structure allows you to isolate platform-specific logic into components or services that can be easily modified or replaced without affecting other parts of the application.

5. Test on Multiple Platforms

- Emulate different devices and operating systems during development to identify and resolve any platform-specific issues early. Automated testing tools like **Selenium** for web apps and **Appium** for mobile apps help in cross-platform testing, reducing manual work.

- Ensure compatibility with different browser versions, operating systems, and devices during testing. This may involve using services like **BrowserStack** or **Sauce Labs** to test your application across a range of real-world devices and browsers.

6. Handle Platform-Specific APIs Separately

- Sometimes, certain features or functionalities (like camera access, GPS, or device storage) require platform-specific APIs. When dealing with such cases, ensure that platform-specific implementations are isolated and only invoked when necessary. You can use libraries or design patterns (like the **Adapter Pattern**) to handle platform-specific code in a way that doesn't clutter your application logic.

Real-World Example: A Company Successfully Building a Web App that Works Across Mobile, Tablet, and Desktop

Consider a company building a **task management web app** that needs to function across mobile, tablet, and desktop devices. The primary goal is to create a consistent, intuitive experience for users, regardless of the device they're using. Here's how they can apply the principles of cross-platform development:

1. **Responsive Design**: The team uses a **responsive front-end framework** like **Bootstrap** or **Material-UI** to ensure the app adjusts its layout based on the device. For example, on a desktop, users see a

sidebar with options to navigate between different sections of the app, while on mobile and tablet, the sidebar collapses into a hamburger menu to save space.

2. **Cross-Platform Frameworks**: The backend is built with **Node.js** for scalability and performance, and it uses **MongoDB** for storing task data. The front-end is developed with **React** to allow for a seamless, component-based structure. This ensures that the app can be scaled across platforms without requiring multiple codebases.

3. **Platform-Specific Features**: The app includes features like **push notifications** for mobile users. Instead of directly integrating platform-specific code into the main app, the team uses a library like **Firebase Cloud Messaging** (FCM) that handles push notifications across both Android and iOS in a unified way.

4. **Testing and Optimization**: The company ensures that their app performs well across devices by testing the layout on different screen sizes using browser developer tools. They use services like **BrowserStack** to test the app across different browsers and devices. They also optimize for performance by reducing JavaScript bundle size and optimizing images, ensuring fast load times even on mobile networks.

This chapter introduced the key principles of cross-platform development, focusing on platform compatibility, device considerations, and UX best practices. We also covered strategies for writing maintainable, scalable code and ensuring consistent experiences across platforms. In the next chapter, we'll explore how APIs and integrations play a crucial role in enabling cross-platform functionality.

CHAPTER 7

DEVELOPING WITH APIS FOR CROSS-PLATFORM PROJECTS

The Importance of APIs in Cross-Platform Software Development

In modern software development, **APIs** (Application Programming Interfaces) play a crucial role, especially in cross-platform projects. APIs allow different software components or systems to communicate with each other, facilitating the integration of diverse platforms. When building cross-platform applications, APIs act as the backbone for enabling communication between different devices, services, and platforms, making them essential for delivering a seamless user experience.

APIs offer several key benefits for cross-platform development:

1. **Consistency Across Platforms**:

o APIs abstract the backend functionality from the front-end user interfaces, allowing different platforms (e.g., mobile, web, desktop) to interact with the same backend services. This ensures that no matter which platform the user is on, they are accessing the same data and services.

2. **Simplified Data Sharing**:

o APIs provide a structured way for apps on different platforms to access shared data. Whether it's user data, app settings, or media files, APIs ensure that information can be retrieved or updated consistently across all devices without needing to replicate data storage for each platform.

3. **Faster Development Cycles**:

o By separating the front-end from the back-end, APIs allow developers to work on both independently. The back-end team can focus on building and optimizing APIs while front-end developers can integrate those APIs into mobile, web, or desktop apps. This parallel development process accelerates the development cycle.

4. **Scalability**:

- o As your cross-platform application grows, APIs allow you to scale your backend systems without impacting the front-end. The backend can be scaled independently by adding more services or resources, while front-end apps can continue interacting with the same APIs.

5. **Third-Party Integrations**:

- o APIs also enable easy integration with third-party services, such as payment gateways, social media platforms, analytics tools, and more. This allows your cross-platform app to leverage external functionality, enriching the user experience without building everything from scratch.

How to Build and Integrate RESTful APIs

REST (Representational State Transfer) is one of the most commonly used architectural styles for designing networked applications. RESTful APIs are easy to use, scalable, and platform-agnostic, making them perfect for cross-platform development. Here's how to build and integrate RESTful APIs into your projects:

1. Building a RESTful API

To create a RESTful API, you need to define endpoints (URLs) that perform different actions on the data, such as retrieving, creating, updating, or deleting resources (CRUD operations). Each endpoint typically corresponds to an HTTP method:

- **GET**: Used to retrieve data from the server.
- **POST**: Used to send data to the server to create a new resource.

- **PUT**: Used to update an existing resource.

- **DELETE**: Used to remove a resource.

Here's a simple example of how to create a RESTful API using **Flask** (a Python web framework) for a to-do list app.

python

Copy

```python
from flask import Flask, jsonify, request

app = Flask(__name__)

# Sample data for tasks
tasks = [
    {"id": 1, "title": "Learn Python", "done": False},
    {"id": 2, "title": "Build an app", "done": True}
]

@app.route('/tasks', methods=['GET'])
def get_tasks():
```

```
    return jsonify({"tasks": tasks})


@app.route('/tasks/<int:task_id>',
methods=['GET'])
def get_task(task_id):
    task = next((task for task in tasks if
task["id"] == task_id), None)
    return jsonify({"task": task}) if task else
("Task not found", 404)


@app.route('/tasks', methods=['POST'])
def create_task():
    new_task = request.get_json()
    tasks.append(new_task)
    return jsonify({"task": new_task}), 201


@app.route('/tasks/<int:task_id>',
methods=['PUT'])
def update_task(task_id):
    task = next((task for task in tasks if
task["id"] == task_id), None)
    if task:
```

```
        task_data = request.get_json()

        task.update(task_data)

        return jsonify({"task": task})

    return ("Task not found", 404)


@app.route('/tasks/<int:task_id>',

methods=['DELETE'])

def delete_task(task_id):

    task = next((task for task in tasks if
task["id"] == task_id), None)

    if task:

        tasks.remove(task)

        return ('', 204)

    return ("Task not found", 404)


if __name__ == '__main__':

    app.run(debug=True)
```

Explanation:

- This simple API allows you to retrieve, create, update, and delete tasks. The API is exposed through URLs like

`/tasks` for listing all tasks and `/tasks/<id>` for managing individual tasks.

- `GET /tasks` returns all tasks, `POST /tasks` creates a new task, `PUT /tasks/<id>` updates an existing task, and `DELETE /tasks/<id>` deletes a task.

2. Integrating the API into Your App

Once the API is built, you can integrate it into your front-end application. Let's consider integrating this API into a mobile app using **React Native** for Android and iOS.

Example: Fetching Tasks from the API in a React Native App

```javascript
Copy
import React, { useState, useEffect } from
'react';
import { View, Text, Button, FlatList } from
'react-native';
```

```
const App = () => {

  const [tasks, setTasks] = useState([]);


  // Fetch tasks from the API

  useEffect(() => {

    fetch('http://<YOUR_SERVER_IP>:5000/tasks')

      .then(response => response.json())

      .then(data => setTasks(data.tasks));

  }, []);


  return (

    <View>

      <Text>My To-Do List</Text>

      <FlatList

        data={tasks}

        keyExtractor={(item)                    =>
item.id.toString()}

        renderItem={({ item }) => (

          <View>

            <Text>{item.title}</Text>

            <Text>{item.done   ?   'Completed'   :
'Pending'}</Text>
```

```
      </View>

       )}

     />

     <Button title="Add Task" onPress={() => {/*
Add task functionality */}} />

    </View>

  );

};


export default App;
```

Explanation:

- In the above example, the `fetch()` function makes a GET request to the API to retrieve the list of tasks and displays them in the mobile app.

- The mobile app communicates with the backend via the RESTful API and renders the task data on the screen.

- You can extend this example to include features like adding, updating, or deleting tasks using the POST, PUT, and DELETE methods on the API.

3. Handling Authentication and Security

When building cross-platform apps that interact with APIs, it's essential to consider security and authentication. You should implement secure methods to protect user data, especially when dealing with sensitive information like user credentials. Common methods include:

- **JWT (JSON Web Tokens)** for stateless authentication.
- **OAuth** for third-party integrations (e.g., Google, Facebook).
- **HTTPS** for secure communication.

Real-World Example: Connecting a Mobile App to a Back-End Service via an API

Imagine a company building a **fitness tracking app** that allows users to log workouts and monitor their progress. The mobile app (built using **React Native**) needs to communicate with a backend server to store and retrieve user workout data. Here's how the company might implement this:

1. **Backend**: The backend is built using **Flask** and exposes a RESTful API to manage workouts. The API provides endpoints for adding new workouts, viewing a list of workouts, and updating workout details.

2. **Mobile App**: The mobile app uses **React Native** to make HTTP requests to the API to retrieve workout data. When the user logs a new workout, the app sends a POST request to the API to store the data on the backend.

3. **Authentication**: The app uses **JWT** for user authentication. When the user logs in, the backend sends a token, which the mobile app stores and includes in subsequent requests to access protected endpoints.

This architecture ensures that the app works consistently across different platforms (iOS and Android) while relying on a single backend service to manage data.

This chapter provided a comprehensive overview of the role of APIs in cross-platform development. We discussed how to build and integrate RESTful APIs and provided a real-world example of connecting a mobile app to a back-end service. In the next chapter, we'll look at how to design a user interface that works seamlessly across different platforms.

CHAPTER 8

UI/UX DESIGN IN CROSS-PLATFORM DEVELOPMENT

Designing a User Interface That Works Across Different Platforms

User interface (UI) and user experience (UX) design are critical to the success of any cross-platform application. While the goal is to maintain a consistent experience across all platforms, it's essential to account for differences in platform guidelines, screen sizes, input methods, and performance. The design should feel native to each platform while maintaining a unified look and feel across mobile, tablet, desktop, and web platforms.

Here are some key considerations for designing an effective cross-platform user interface:

1. Platform-Specific Guidelines

- **Mobile vs. Desktop**: The design needs to adapt to different interaction methods. On mobile, users interact primarily through touch, requiring larger buttons, touch-friendly navigation, and swipe actions. On desktop, users typically interact with a mouse and keyboard, so the design may include more detailed menus, toolbars, and keyboard shortcuts.

- **Native Design Elements**: Each platform has its own design language and UI conventions (e.g., Material Design for Android, Human Interface Guidelines for iOS). While it's essential to maintain a consistent brand identity, it's also crucial to respect these platform-specific guidelines to give users a familiar experience. For example, Android apps often use bottom navigation bars, while iOS apps may prefer tab bars at the bottom or top.

- **Consistency Across Devices**: Ensuring a consistent experience across platforms can be challenging due to varying screen sizes, resolutions, and form factors. A good cross-platform UI design should scale appropriately, providing an optimal experience on mobile, tablet, and desktop devices.

2. Responsive and Adaptive Design

- **Responsive Design**: Responsive design allows the interface to adjust dynamically based on the screen size, orientation, and resolution. This ensures that your app will look great on any device, from small smartphones to large desktop monitors.

- **Adaptive Design**: Adaptive design involves creating multiple layouts or templates for different devices. For example, you might design a mobile-specific layout for small screens and a tablet or desktop-specific layout for larger screens. Tools like CSS media queries, Flexbox, and frameworks like Bootstrap make it easier to implement responsive designs.

3. User-Centered Design

- Cross-platform UI/UX design should prioritize the user experience, focusing on the needs, preferences, and behaviors of the target audience. Designing with empathy allows you to create intuitive and easy-to-navigate interfaces that improve user satisfaction across platforms.

- Use user feedback and testing to refine the design. Cross-platform apps often require extra testing to ensure usability across all devices. Regular testing across devices helps identify potential issues related to platform-specific quirks and UI scaling.

Tools and Frameworks for Building Responsive User Interfaces

Several tools and frameworks are designed to streamline the process of building cross-platform user interfaces. These tools allow developers to create responsive UIs without needing to start from scratch for each platform.

1. Xamarin

- **Xamarin** is a powerful cross-platform development framework for building mobile apps for Android, iOS, and Windows using C#. It enables developers to create native UIs with shared code across platforms.

- **Xamarin.Forms** is a UI toolkit within Xamarin that allows for the creation of native user interfaces across iOS, Android, and Windows Phone with a shared codebase. Xamarin provides device-specific functionality, but the majority of the UI can be built with Xamarin.Forms, ensuring consistency across platforms.

- Xamarin also allows developers to use native controls when necessary, offering flexibility in adapting to platform-specific UI conventions while maintaining a unified experience.

2. Kivy

- **Kivy** is an open-source Python library for building multi-touch applications, particularly suited for mobile and desktop applications. It's a great option for developers who prefer Python over Java or C#.

- Kivy offers a wide range of UI components, such as buttons, text inputs, sliders, and navigation menus, all designed to work across Android, iOS, Windows, Linux, and macOS. The library is flexible and supports custom widget creation, which is essential for building complex, interactive UIs.

3. Flutter

- **Flutter**, created by Google, is a UI toolkit for building natively compiled applications for mobile, web, and desktop from a single codebase. It uses the **Dart** programming language and allows developers to create rich, responsive, and highly customizable UIs.

- Flutter provides a set of pre-designed widgets that mimic native design languages (Material Design for Android and Cupertino for iOS), ensuring the app feels native on each platform. Flutter also includes a powerful hot-reload feature, making it easy to experiment with UI designs and see real-time changes.

4. React Native

- **React Native** is a popular JavaScript framework for building native mobile applications. With React Native, developers use JavaScript and React components to create apps that work on both iOS and Android.

- It uses a "bridge" to interact with native APIs, allowing developers to create fully native UIs while sharing code across platforms. React Native also allows the use of platform-specific components when necessary to ensure adherence to platform-specific guidelines.

5. Electron

- **Electron** allows developers to build desktop applications using web technologies such as HTML, CSS, and JavaScript. It combines Chromium and Node.js, enabling the development of cross-platform desktop apps that can run on Windows, macOS, and Linux.

- Electron is ideal for building cross-platform desktop applications that share a codebase with web apps. Popular applications like Slack and Visual Studio Code have been built using Electron.

Real-World Example: Designing a Unified Interface for a Financial Application

Imagine a company developing a **financial tracking application** for users to manage their personal finances across multiple devices (mobile, tablet, and desktop). The app needs to provide users with an intuitive, consistent experience, regardless of the device they use.

Here's how the design process might unfold:

1. **Understanding the Requirements**:
   - The company identifies the main features of the app, such as tracking income and expenses, creating financial reports, setting budget goals, and visualizing spending trends.
   - The target audience includes people who are frequently on the go (mobile users), as well as

people who prefer managing their finances on a larger screen (desktop and tablet users).

2. **Designing with Platform Guidelines**:

   o For **mobile devices**, the design should focus on simplicity and ease of use. Large buttons, straightforward navigation, and intuitive charting components are key to delivering a user-friendly experience.

   o For **desktop** devices, more detailed information and additional features like keyboard shortcuts and drag-and-drop functionality can be introduced. The desktop layout can take advantage of the larger screen to display more data, such as multiple financial charts or detailed reports.

3. **Responsive Layout**:

   o The app is designed using **Flutter** to ensure a responsive layout that adapts seamlessly between mobile, tablet, and desktop devices.

- o For mobile devices, the app uses a tab bar for easy access to different sections (Home, Transactions, Budget, Reports), while on tablets and desktops, the layout features a sidebar for quicker navigation and the ability to see more content at once.

- o The financial charts and reports are displayed as scalable widgets that adjust their size depending on the device's screen size, ensuring readability on both small and large screens.

4. **Using Cross-Platform UI Frameworks**:

- o The app uses **Flutter** to create a unified design that mimics the native feel of Android (Material Design) and iOS (Cupertino) for mobile devices. For the desktop, the app leverages Flutter's **desktop support** to maintain consistency while optimizing the UI for larger screens.

- o The app uses platform-specific widgets when necessary (e.g., native date pickers or chart libraries) to maintain the app's native feel across platforms.

5. **Testing Across Devices**:

   o Once the initial design is complete, the app undergoes testing across mobile, tablet, and desktop devices to ensure that the user interface functions correctly, scales properly, and adheres to platform-specific guidelines.

   o Feedback from users is gathered to refine the design, focusing on usability improvements and platform-specific adjustments.

In this chapter, we explored the principles of UI/UX design in cross-platform development, including the importance of designing with platform guidelines in mind, responsive and adaptive design, and using the right tools and frameworks. We also provided a real-world example of designing a unified interface for a financial tracking application that works seamlessly across mobile, tablet, and desktop devices. In the next chapter, we'll dive into how cross-platform libraries and frameworks help optimize performance and functionality across platforms.

CHAPTER 9

CROSS-PLATFORM LIBRARIES AND FRAMEWORKS

Introduction to Popular Cross-Platform Libraries

Cross-platform libraries and frameworks allow developers to write one codebase that can be used on multiple platforms, such as Android, iOS, Windows, macOS, and the web. These tools help streamline the development process by abstracting platform-specific details and enabling developers to focus on building features and functionality.

Here's an overview of some popular cross-platform libraries and frameworks:

1. React Native

- **Overview**: **React Native** is a widely-used JavaScript framework developed by Facebook for building mobile apps that run on both Android and iOS. It allows developers to use JavaScript and React components to create mobile applications with native performance.

- **Key Features**:
  - o Reusable components: React Native allows developers to write components that can be reused across platforms, providing a unified codebase for both Android and iOS.
  - o Native performance: React Native uses a bridge to interact with native APIs, allowing for native-like performance, which makes it ideal for mobile apps that require high performance.
  - o Large community and ecosystem: React Native has a large community, meaning many pre-built components and libraries are available to speed up development.
- **Use Cases**:
  - o Mobile apps (Android and iOS) such as Facebook, Instagram, and Airbnb.

o Ideal for apps that require smooth user interactions and complex UI elements.

2. Xamarin

- **Overview**: **Xamarin** is a Microsoft-backed framework for building cross-platform mobile applications using C#. It enables developers to write native Android, iOS, and Windows apps with a shared codebase, using the same language and tools for all platforms.

- **Key Features**:

    o Native UI components: Xamarin allows for full access to platform-specific APIs, enabling developers to use native UI components for each platform while still sharing code across devices.

    o Xamarin.Forms: A powerful library for building cross-platform UIs that can be shared between Android, iOS, and Windows, making it easy to create unified apps.

    o Integration with the .NET ecosystem: Xamarin integrates well with Microsoft's tools and cloud

108

services, such as Azure, for app deployment and management.

- **Use Cases**:
  - o Mobile apps for businesses that are heavily integrated into the Microsoft ecosystem.
  - o Applications that require native performance and platform-specific functionalities.

3. Kivy

- **Overview**: **Kivy** is an open-source Python framework for building multi-touch applications that work across multiple platforms, including Android, iOS, Windows, macOS, and Linux. It is especially popular for applications with complex touch interfaces or applications that require support for gestures, swiping, or multitouch.

- **Key Features**:
  - o Highly customizable UI: Kivy allows developers to design highly interactive and custom user

interfaces with widgets that support multi-touch, gestures, and other advanced inputs.

- o Cross-platform support: Kivy applications can be deployed on Android, iOS, Windows, macOS, and Linux with minimal changes.

- o Python-based: Since Kivy is built in Python, it is especially attractive to Python developers who want to create mobile or desktop apps without learning other languages like Java or C#.

- **Use Cases**:
  - o Interactive mobile apps with multi-touch support (e.g., games or graphical applications).
  - o Ideal for rapid prototyping and applications that need to be developed quickly.

4. Flutter

- **Overview**: **Flutter** is a UI toolkit from Google that enables developers to build natively compiled applications for mobile, web, and desktop from a single codebase. It uses the Dart programming language and is

110

designed to provide a rich, high-performance UI with smooth animations.

- **Key Features**:
  - o Single codebase for mobile, web, and desktop apps.
  - o Widgets for both Android (Material Design) and iOS (Cupertino) for platform-specific UI elements.
  - o Hot reload feature that allows developers to instantly see changes in the code during development.

- **Use Cases**:
  - o Building apps that need to run on Android, iOS, web, and desktop.
  - o Ideal for applications with rich UIs, smooth animations, and high performance.

Choosing the Right Framework for Different Types of Projects

Choosing the right cross-platform framework depends on several factors, such as project requirements, team expertise, and performance considerations. Here are some guidelines for selecting the most suitable framework for your project:

1. **For Mobile-Only Apps**:
   o If your primary goal is to build a mobile app, frameworks like **React Native** and **Flutter** are ideal choices. Both provide native-like performance with the added benefit of a shared codebase for Android and iOS, allowing for rapid development.
   o **React Native** is a good choice if your team is already familiar with JavaScript and React, as it allows them to leverage existing skills.
   o **Flutter** is perfect if you need a highly customizable UI with smooth animations and want to extend your app to the web or desktop in the future.

2. **For Enterprise-Level Apps with .NET Integration**:

112

- o **Xamarin** is an excellent choice for apps that need to be deeply integrated with the Microsoft ecosystem, including Azure services, Active Directory, and other enterprise solutions.

- o Xamarin's native performance and access to platform-specific APIs make it a great option for enterprise mobile apps.

3. **For Apps with Complex UI or Multi-Touch Support**:

- o If your app requires complex touch gestures or custom UI elements, **Kivy** might be the best framework. It's especially suited for applications like games or apps with advanced graphical features.

- o **Flutter** is also a good choice for high-performance UIs and smooth animations.

4. **For Rapid Prototyping or Simple Apps**:

- o **React Native** and **Kivy** are both great options for quickly building and iterating on prototypes or smaller apps. React Native's large community of pre-built libraries can help you speed up development, while Kivy's simplicity and flexibility make it a good choice for prototyping in Python.

Real-World Example: How a Company Used Xamarin to Build a Successful Mobile App

Let's consider a real-world example where a **financial services company** used **Xamarin** to build a successful mobile app. The app allows users to manage their finances, track investments, and receive personalized financial advice. Here's how they approached the development process:

1. **Objective**:

   o The company wanted to create a mobile app that could be used by customers across both Android and iOS devices. It needed to have a native look and feel, with performance that was fast enough to handle complex financial data and secure transactions.

o Additionally, the company wanted to ensure a unified experience for both platforms while reducing development and maintenance costs by sharing the codebase.

2. **Choosing Xamarin**:

o The development team chose **Xamarin** because it allowed them to write most of the application logic in C# and share the codebase between Android and iOS. Xamarin's integration with the .NET ecosystem was a strong selling point, as the company was already using Microsoft technologies for their backend services.

o Xamarin.Forms was used to create a common UI across both platforms, while the team also utilized Xamarin's ability to write platform-specific code for certain features that required native APIs, such as financial transactions and biometric login.

3. **Development Process**:

115

o The team designed the user interface with Xamarin.Forms, ensuring that the app was responsive and looked native on both Android and iOS. They utilized Xamarin's platform-specific APIs to integrate with Android's fingerprint authentication and iOS's Face ID.

o The app was connected to a cloud-based backend for secure data storage, and Xamarin's integration with Azure made it easy to implement secure authentication and manage user data.

4. **Outcome**:

o The app was successfully launched on both Android and iOS with a shared codebase, reducing development time and costs. The app received positive feedback from users due to its native performance and smooth UI.

o The company was able to quickly iterate on the app based on user feedback and introduced new features across both platforms simultaneously, thanks to Xamarin's cross-platform capabilities.

116

In this chapter, we explored popular cross-platform libraries and frameworks like **React Native**, **Xamarin**, **Kivy**, and **Flutter**, and discussed how to choose the right framework for different types of projects. We also provided a real-world example of how a company used **Xamarin** to build a successful mobile app. In the next chapter, we'll discuss how to manage data across multiple platforms and ensure synchronization.

CHAPTER 10

MOBILE DEVELOPMENT WITH PYTHON AND C#

Building Cross-Platform Mobile Applications Using Python and C#

Mobile development has evolved significantly, and with the rise of cross-platform development, developers can now build mobile applications that run on both **iOS** and **Android** using a single codebase. This eliminates the need to develop separate applications for each platform, saving time and resources. **Python** and **C#** are two powerful languages that allow for efficient cross-platform mobile app development.

Python and C# offer different approaches and frameworks for mobile development, each with its strengths. In this chapter, we'll dive into how both languages can be used to develop cross-platform mobile apps and explore some of the popular frameworks available.

1. Building Cross-Platform Mobile Applications with Python

Python is widely known for its simplicity and ease of use, but it's also capable of building powerful mobile apps using several frameworks that provide cross-platform support. Although Python isn't traditionally used for mobile development, frameworks like **Kivy** and **BeeWare** make it a strong contender for mobile app development.

Kivy

- **Kivy** is an open-source Python library for developing multi-touch applications. It's highly customizable, allowing developers to create mobile apps with a wide range of touch gestures, which is especially useful for mobile devices.

- **Key Features**:
    - **Cross-platform**: Kivy supports Android, iOS, Windows, Linux, and macOS.

119

- o **Multitouch and Gestures**: Kivy provides powerful support for multitouch and gestures, making it ideal for mobile and interactive applications.

- o **Widgets and UI**: Kivy comes with a variety of UI elements and customizable widgets to build rich mobile interfaces.

- o **Python-based**: Developers familiar with Python can create mobile apps without needing to learn additional languages like Java or Swift.

Example:

```python
Copy
from kivy.app import App
from kivy.uix.button import Button

class MyApp(App):
    def build(self):
        return Button(text='Hello, Kivy!')
```

```
if __name__ == '__main__':
    MyApp().run()
```

In this example, Kivy creates a simple button with the text "Hello, Kivy!". The code can run on Android, iOS, or desktop platforms.

BeeWare

- **BeeWare** is a collection of tools and libraries for building native user interfaces in Python. Unlike Kivy, BeeWare focuses more on creating apps that integrate tightly with the platform's native APIs, providing a more "native" look and feel.

- **Key Features**:

  o **Native Widgets**: BeeWare allows you to use native widgets, giving your app a truly native user experience across platforms.

  o **Cross-platform**: BeeWare supports Android, iOS, macOS, Linux, and Windows.

121

- o **Widget Library**: The Toga library within BeeWare helps create the user interface for apps that can run on multiple platforms.

Example:

```python
Copy
from toga import App, Button, Box

class MyApp(App):
    def startup(self):
        box = Box()
        button = Button('Hello, BeeWare!',
on_press=self.say_hello)
        box.add(button)
        self.main_window                    =
self.main_window = toga.MainWindow()
        self.main_window.content = box
        self.main_window.show()

    def say_hello(self, widget):
```

```
    print("Hello, BeeWare!")


def main():

    return MyApp()


if __name__ == '__main__':

    main().run()
```

2. Building Cross-Platform Mobile Applications with C#

C# has strong support for mobile app development, particularly through the **Xamarin** framework. Xamarin allows developers to create fully native apps using a shared codebase in C#. Xamarin is a great option for developers with experience in the Microsoft ecosystem.

Xamarin

- **Xamarin** is a Microsoft-supported framework that allows developers to build mobile apps for **Android** and **iOS** using C# and the .NET framework.

- **Key Features**:

    o **Single Codebase**: Xamarin allows you to write most of the app in C#, and it will run on both iOS and Android. Some platform-specific code may still be necessary, but a large part of the codebase can be shared across platforms.

    o **Native Performance**: Xamarin provides access to native APIs and can produce native user interfaces, ensuring that the app performs well on both platforms.

    o **Xamarin.Forms**: Xamarin.Forms is a framework that allows you to design a single user interface for multiple platforms. Xamarin also allows for platform-specific customization when needed.

Example:

```csharp
Copy
using Xamarin.Forms;

public class App : Application
{
    public App()
    {
        var button = new Button
        {
            Text = "Hello, Xamarin!"
        };

        button.Clicked += (sender, args) =>
        {
            button.Text = "Hello, C#!";
        };

        MainPage = new ContentPage
```

125

```
        {

            Content = new StackLayout

            {

                Children = { button }

            }

        };

    }

}
```

In this example, a simple button is created that changes text when clicked. The code can be shared between iOS and Android, and Xamarin will handle compiling the code into the appropriate format for each platform.

3. Choosing the Right Framework for Different Types of Projects

When choosing the right framework for a mobile app, developers need to consider several factors, including the type of app, performance requirements, and the development team's expertise. Here's a comparison of when to choose each framework:

Kivy:

- **Best For**: Interactive, multitouch applications or quick prototypes.
- **Pros**: Fast development, customizable widgets, Python-based.
- **Cons**: Limited to certain types of apps (e.g., graphics-heavy apps), less native-looking compared to Xamarin or BeeWare.

BeeWare:

- **Best For**: Apps that need to integrate deeply with the operating system and provide a native UI experience.
- **Pros**: Native look and feel, Python-based, uses native widgets.
- **Cons**: Smaller community, limited features compared to other frameworks like Xamarin or Flutter.

Xamarin:

- **Best For**: Business or enterprise apps that require high performance and integration with the Microsoft ecosystem.

- **Pros**: Full access to platform-specific APIs, native performance, integrates well with .NET and Azure.

- **Cons**: Larger app size, potentially steep learning curve for new developers.

4. Real-World Example: Developing a Cross-Platform App for Both iOS and Android

Consider a **fitness tracker app** that needs to run on both Android and iOS. The app will track users' steps, calories, and workouts, and display graphs of their progress. The company decides to use **Xamarin** for this project for several reasons: it's a Microsoft-based company, they're comfortable with C#, and they want to integrate the app with their Azure services.

1. **Designing the App**:

   o The app will feature a home screen with a summary of the user's activity, a button to start workouts, and a settings page to manage user preferences.

   o Using **Xamarin.Forms**, the development team creates a unified UI that will work across both iOS and Android devices.

2. **Backend Integration**:

   o The fitness data is stored in a cloud database (e.g., Azure), and the app syncs data from the cloud when the user opens the app. The backend is built with **ASP.NET Core** and communicates with the app via RESTful APIs.

3. **Using Platform-Specific Features**:

   o The team uses Xamarin's platform-specific APIs to access the device's pedometer on both iOS and Android to track steps. They also integrate with **Google Fit** (Android) and **HealthKit** (iOS) to retrieve more detailed health data.

4. **Testing and Deployment**:

   o The team tests the app on both Android and iOS devices to ensure that the user interface scales properly and performs well. They use Xamarin's integrated tools for debugging and profiling to ensure a smooth experience.

5. **Outcome**:

   o The app is successfully developed with a single codebase, and it is deployed to both the **Google Play Store** and **Apple App Store**. The app performs well on both platforms, and users report a consistent experience on Android and iOS.

In this chapter, we explored how to develop cross-platform mobile apps using **Python** and **C#**, focusing on frameworks like **Kivy**, **BeeWare**, and **Xamarin**. We also discussed how to choose the right framework for different types of projects and provided a real-world example of developing a fitness tracker app for both iOS and Android. In the next chapter, we will delve into how to manage data across multiple platforms and ensure synchronization.

CHAPTER 11

SECURITY IN CROSS-PLATFORM DEVELOPMENT

Ensuring Robust Security Practices When Developing Cross-Platform Applications

Security is one of the most critical aspects of any software development process, especially when building cross-platform applications that may handle sensitive data. Whether the app is dealing with financial transactions, personal data, or enterprise-level information, ensuring robust security practices is crucial to prevent breaches and protect user privacy.

Cross-platform development introduces a set of unique security challenges due to the variety of platforms involved (Android, iOS, Windows, macOS, and web). These platforms have different security features, libraries, and behaviors, which need to be taken into account during the development process.

Here are several key practices for ensuring robust security in cross-platform applications:

1. Data Encryption

- **Encrypting Sensitive Data**: Encrypt sensitive data both at rest (on the device) and in transit (while being transferred over the network). This ensures that even if an attacker gains access to the device or intercepts the network traffic, they cannot read the data.
  - Use **AES (Advanced Encryption Standard)** for encrypting data at rest.
  - For data in transit, always use **HTTPS (SSL/TLS)** to secure communications between the client and the server. **SSL certificates** should be properly managed and updated.
- **Example**: Encrypt passwords using **PBKDF2, bcrypt**, or **Argon2** before storing them on the server.

2. Authentication and Authorization

- **Secure Authentication**: Implement strong authentication mechanisms, such as multi-factor authentication (MFA) or biometric authentication (fingerprint or Face ID) for mobile apps. Use industry-standard authentication protocols like **OAuth 2.0** or **OpenID Connect** to enable secure user authentication across different platforms.

- **Token-Based Authentication**: Use **JWT (JSON Web Tokens)** for secure token-based authentication. JWT is a secure and stateless way to authenticate users without needing to store session data on the server.

- **Access Control**: Implement proper access control measures, ensuring that users only have access to data and functionality they are authorized to use. Always follow the principle of least privilege.

3. Secure Storage

- Use platform-specific secure storage solutions to store sensitive data like API keys, passwords, and tokens. For example:

  o **iOS**: Use **Keychain Services** to securely store credentials and sensitive data.

  o **Android**: Use **Keystore** for secure key storage and **EncryptedSharedPreferences** to store sensitive data securely.

  o **Cross-platform**: Utilize libraries like **Secure Storage** in Xamarin or **EncryptedSharedPreferences** in React Native to handle secure storage of data across platforms.

4. Regular Updates and Patch Management

- Ensure that both the app and its dependencies are regularly updated to address new vulnerabilities. This includes updating third-party libraries, frameworks, and platform-specific SDKs that the app relies on.

- Regularly apply **security patches** to the server-side infrastructure, including web servers, databases, and cloud services.

5. Secure APIs

- When building cross-platform apps, most communication happens through APIs. Ensure that the APIs used for client-server communication are secured properly:

    o **Rate Limiting**: Prevent abuse by limiting the number of requests a user or system can make within a certain time period.

    o **Input Validation**: Always validate inputs to prevent attacks like SQL injection, XSS (Cross-Site Scripting), and CSRF (Cross-Site Request Forgery).

    o **Authorization**: Ensure that APIs require proper authentication and authorization before access is granted to sensitive resources. Use **OAuth2.0** for secure API authentication.

6. Platform-Specific Security Considerations

- Each platform has its own unique security features and vulnerabilities. It's essential to be aware of these when developing cross-platform applications. For instance:

  o **Android**: Android apps can be reverse-engineered, so sensitive information like API keys and tokens should not be stored in plain text within the app. Use the Android Keystore system to securely store sensitive data.

  o **iOS**: iOS apps are sandboxed for security, but developers should still follow best practices to protect sensitive data and prevent unauthorized access.

  o **Web**: Web applications face additional challenges such as Cross-Origin Resource Sharing (CORS) issues and browser vulnerabilities, so developers must ensure their web APIs are secure and protected against common attacks like XSS and CSRF.

Addressing Platform-Specific Security Concerns and How to Mitigate Them

Different platforms come with distinct security features, but they also introduce unique security risks. Below are some common platform-specific security concerns and how to address them:

1. Android Security Concerns

- **App Reverse Engineering**: Android apps are susceptible to reverse engineering due to the open-source nature of the platform. To mitigate this risk, use code obfuscation tools like **ProGuard** or **R8** to make it harder for attackers to reverse-engineer the app.

- **Data Leakage**: Sensitive data may leak through various channels like logs, third-party libraries, or even unsecured storage. To prevent this, always store sensitive data in the **Android Keystore** and ensure that it is properly encrypted.

- **App Permissions**: Ensure the app only requests the permissions it absolutely needs. Over-requesting permissions can expose the app to potential attacks.

2. iOS Security Concerns

- **Jailbreaking**: Jailbroken devices bypass Apple's built-in security mechanisms, which can expose your app to malicious activities. Use **anti-jailbreaking libraries** and check whether the device is jailbroken during app launch to mitigate this risk.

- **Data Protection**: Ensure that sensitive data is protected using **iOS Keychain Services** and **Data Protection API**. Use **App Transport Security (ATS)** to enforce secure communication over HTTPS.

- **Code Injection**: iOS is more secure than Android in terms of code injection, but it's still crucial to follow best practices to protect against such attacks. Always ensure the integrity of your app with **App Attestation** and **Runtime Protection** mechanisms.

3. Web Security Concerns

- **Cross-Site Scripting (XSS)**: XSS is a common web vulnerability where malicious scripts are injected into web pages. Prevent this by validating all user inputs and using output encoding techniques.

- **Cross-Site Request Forgery (CSRF)**: CSRF attacks trick the user into making unwanted requests. Use **CSRF tokens** to protect against this kind of attack.

- **Session Management**: Ensure that session management is handled securely by using **Secure HTTP Cookies**, implementing **SameSite cookies** to protect against cross-site attacks, and utilizing **secure logout** mechanisms.

Real-World Example: Securing a Cross-Platform Banking App

Let's take the example of a **banking app** that needs to operate securely across both **iOS** and **Android** platforms. The app allows users to check their account balance, transfer funds, and view transaction history. Due to the sensitivity of financial data, ensuring top-notch security is a top priority.

1. Encryption of Sensitive Data

- All sensitive user data, such as login credentials, account information, and transaction details, is **encrypted** both at rest and in transit.

- On the client side, sensitive data is stored in **Keychain (iOS)** and **Keystore (Android)**, both of which are secure storage solutions provided by their respective platforms.

- Data in transit is encrypted using **HTTPS (SSL/TLS)**, ensuring that communication between the app and the server is secure.

2. Authentication and Authorization

- The banking app uses **multi-factor authentication (MFA)**, requiring both a password and a one-time code sent via SMS or email. This adds an extra layer of security to user accounts.

- The app uses **OAuth 2.0** for secure token-based authentication when communicating with the backend server, and **JWT (JSON Web Tokens)** for maintaining user sessions.

3. Secure API Integration

- The app interacts with a backend API to retrieve account information and initiate fund transfers. All API calls are secured using **OAuth 2.0** authentication tokens and **rate limiting** to prevent abuse.

- The backend uses **input validation**, **output encoding**, and **SQL injection prevention** techniques to secure the app against common attacks.

4. Platform-Specific Considerations

- On Android, the app uses **ProGuard** for code obfuscation to make it difficult for attackers to reverse-engineer the app.

- On iOS, the app uses **App Transport Security (ATS)** to enforce secure communications and **Keychain Services** for securely storing user credentials and financial data.

5. Regular Updates

- The development team ensures that both the app and backend systems are regularly updated to patch any known security vulnerabilities. They also follow security best practices and guidelines provided by both Google and Apple.

In this chapter, we've explored key security practices for cross-platform development, including data encryption, authentication, secure storage, and platform-specific considerations. We also provided a real-world example of how to secure a banking app, ensuring that sensitive financial data is protected on both Android and iOS platforms. In the next chapter, we'll look at how to optimize cross-platform apps for performance.

CHAPTER 12

PERFORMANCE OPTIMIZATION FOR CROSS-PLATFORM APPS

Best Practices for Optimizing the Performance of Cross-Platform

Applications

Performance is a critical aspect of any cross-platform application, especially as the complexity of apps increases. Slow load times, unresponsiveness, and inefficient resource usage can lead to poor user experiences and low user retention. In cross-platform development, performance optimization becomes even more crucial because you need to ensure that the app runs efficiently across various devices, operating systems, and platforms.

Here are some key best practices to optimize the performance of cross-platform applications:

1. Optimize App Startup Time

- **Lazy Loading**: Instead of loading all resources at once, load essential components first and defer others. This reduces the initial startup time and improves the user experience. For instance, only load critical UI elements initially, and defer non-essential components like images or additional screens until they are needed.

- **Efficient Asset Management**: Compress and optimize images, icons, and other assets to reduce their size. Large files can significantly slow down the app, especially on mobile devices. Use formats like WebP for images and ensure that your app doesn't load high-resolution assets unnecessarily.

- **Asynchronous Initialization**: Make use of asynchronous operations when initializing components or fetching data. By allowing the app to run non-blocking tasks in the background, users won't experience delays when launching the app.

2. Efficient Memory Management

- **Avoid Memory Leaks**: Memory leaks can drastically affect performance, especially in mobile apps. In languages like **Python** and **C#**, ensure that memory management is handled properly, and avoid holding references to objects unnecessarily. Use automatic garbage collection in C# (via **.NET Core**) and make sure to explicitly release objects when they're no longer needed in Python.

- **Memory Profiling**: Regularly monitor the memory usage of your app to identify any spikes or unusual consumption patterns. This can help detect unnecessary object retention or inefficient resource usage.

3. Optimize UI Rendering

- **Efficient Rendering**: Avoid complex UI operations on the main thread. In most mobile and desktop platforms, the main thread is responsible for rendering UI updates, so performing heavy calculations or I/O operations on the main thread will make the app feel sluggish.

- **Use Hardware Acceleration**: Use hardware-accelerated features when available, especially for animations and rendering. Both **Flutter** and **React Native** utilize GPU acceleration for smooth animations, which is essential for building responsive UIs on mobile devices.

- **Virtualization**: For apps displaying large lists or data (e.g., a long list of transactions or images), consider using techniques like **virtualization** or **pagination** to load only the items visible on the screen, reducing the amount of data that needs to be rendered and processed.

4. Optimize Network Calls

- **Minimize Network Requests**: Excessive network requests can slow down your app, especially on mobile devices with slower connections. Reduce the number of requests by batching them when possible, caching responses, and avoiding redundant calls.

- **API Performance**: Optimize the performance of your API calls by compressing data, using pagination for large datasets, and avoiding sending unnecessary data. For example, avoid fetching large media files unless needed and use smaller data sets or JSON objects for APIs.

- **Network Caching**: Cache responses from frequent API calls locally (using libraries like **SQLite**, **Realm**, or **SharedPreferences** on mobile devices) to avoid hitting the network on every request.

5. Efficient Cross-Platform Code

- **Optimize Shared Code**: When using a cross-platform framework, ensure that the shared code (i.e., the code that runs across all platforms) is optimized. Avoid platform-specific code that could negatively affect performance on some devices.

- **Native Modules**: Sometimes, it's more efficient to use platform-specific modules or APIs for performance-sensitive tasks, such as heavy computation or accessing hardware resources. Cross-platform frameworks like **Xamarin** and **React Native** allow developers to write platform-specific code when necessary to optimize performance.

6. Use Background Threads and Multithreading

- For resource-intensive tasks such as data processing, consider offloading work to background threads or use **multithreading** to prevent the main thread from being blocked. This ensures that UI updates remain responsive while background tasks run in parallel.

- **Python** and **C#** both support multithreading and asynchronous programming. Use **async/await** patterns in Python and **Task Parallel Library (TPL)** or **async/await** in C# to write non-blocking code.

Profiling and Debugging Tools for Python and C#

To ensure that the optimizations are effective and that performance issues are identified early, developers need to use profiling and debugging tools. These tools help in pinpointing bottlenecks, inefficient operations, and memory leaks.

1. Profiling and Debugging in Python

- **cProfile**: `cProfile` is a built-in Python module used to measure the performance of Python code. It shows where time is being spent in the code and allows developers to optimize performance by identifying slow sections.
  - o Example: Running `python -m cProfile my_script.py` will give you a detailed report on function calls and execution times.
- **Py-Spy**: **Py-Spy** is an easy-to-use sampling profiler for Python that can be run on production systems with minimal overhead. It gives insights into where your Python application spends most of its time.
- **Memory Profiler**: Use the **memory_profiler** package to track memory usage over time, which is essential for detecting memory leaks in your app.
  - o Example: `pip install memory_profiler` and use `@profile` to decorate functions for memory profiling.

150

- **PDB (Python Debugger)**: **PDB** is the built-in interactive debugger for Python. It allows developers to step through code line by line, inspect variables, and evaluate expressions to identify issues.

2. Profiling and Debugging in C#

- **Visual Studio Profiler**: Visual Studio provides a powerful profiling tool that helps developers analyze CPU usage, memory allocation, and network activity within their app. It's ideal for detecting performance bottlenecks in both mobile and desktop apps.

- **Xamarin Profiler**: Xamarin provides its own profiler for debugging mobile apps specifically. It allows you to analyze memory usage, garbage collection, and CPU usage on iOS and Android devices.

- **DotTrace**: **DotTrace** is a profiling tool for .NET applications that helps developers track memory usage, find performance bottlenecks, and optimize the app's performance.

- **Application Insights**: Microsoft's **Application Insights** is a powerful tool for tracking application performance, user behavior, and telemetry data from both mobile and server-side components of your app.

Real-World Example: Improving the Load Times and Responsiveness of a Cross-Platform App

Let's consider a **task management app** developed using **Xamarin** that needs to improve its load times and responsiveness on both iOS and Android.

1. **Initial Problem**:
   o The app experiences slow load times when starting up, especially on older Android devices.
   o The main screen, which shows a list of tasks, takes several seconds to load because of large images and complex UI components.

2. **Optimizing Startup Time**:

o **Lazy Loading**: The app's main screen initially loads only the task titles and other essential information. Images and additional details are fetched asynchronously once the main screen has loaded.

o **Image Optimization**: The app's images are optimized for mobile devices by compressing them and using the **WebP** format to reduce file sizes without sacrificing quality.

o **Asynchronous Initialization**: The app's background services (like syncing with the server) run asynchronously so that they do not block the UI thread during app startup.

3. **Improving UI Rendering**:

o **Virtualization**: The list of tasks is now rendered using Xamarin's **ListView** with virtualization enabled. This ensures that only the visible tasks are rendered at any given time, which greatly improves performance when dealing with large datasets.

    o **Smooth Animations**: Animations for task transitions are simplified, and **GPU acceleration** is used to make transitions smoother.

4. **Reducing API Call Latency**:

    o The app's API calls are optimized to fetch only the essential data when the user first opens the app. Non-essential data is loaded later using background tasks.

    o **Caching**: Data that doesn't change frequently (like task titles) is cached locally to reduce the number of network requests, which significantly improves load times.

5. **Profiling and Monitoring**:

    o Using the **Xamarin Profiler** and **Visual Studio Profiler**, the development team identifies that the app's memory usage is high due to inefficient resource management in certain areas. They implement better memory handling, reducing memory usage by 30%.

6. **Outcome**:

o   The optimizations result in a faster load time (reduced from 5 seconds to 2 seconds) and improved responsiveness across both Android and iOS devices.

o   User feedback improves, as the app now provides a smoother and more responsive experience.

In this chapter, we discussed best practices for optimizing the performance of cross-platform applications, including optimizing load times, improving memory management, and optimizing UI rendering. We also covered profiling and debugging tools for Python and C#, which help identify performance bottlenecks. Finally, we provided a real-world example of improving the load times and responsiveness of a cross-platform task management app. In the next chapter, we'll explore how to integrate cloud services into cross-platform applications.

CHAPTER 14

CLOUD INTEGRATION IN CROSS-PLATFORM DEVELOPMENT

Integrating Cloud Services into Cross-Platform Applications

Cloud integration has become a crucial component in modern software development. By leveraging cloud services, developers can ensure scalability, reliability, and ease of maintenance for cross-platform applications. Cloud platforms provide storage, compute resources, and a variety of managed services that help streamline the development process while reducing the overhead of managing on-premise infrastructure.

Integrating cloud services into cross-platform applications is a powerful way to handle backend operations like user authentication, data storage, real-time communication, analytics, and more. Cloud services enable the app to work seamlessly across different devices, platforms, and operating systems while handling tasks that would be cumbersome or costly to do locally.

Here's how cloud integration typically works for cross-platform apps:

- **Backend as a Service (BaaS)**: Cloud providers offer services like **Firebase** and **AWS Amplify,** which handle backend operations like authentication, database management, and file storage. These services allow developers to focus more on building front-end applications while leaving the complexity of server-side management to the cloud.

- **Serverless Computing**: Services like **AWS Lambda** or **Azure Functions** allow developers to run backend code without managing servers. This reduces the complexity of cloud infrastructure management and helps to scale applications automatically as demand increases.

- **Real-Time Data**: Cloud platforms enable real-time updates and communication between the client and the server, essential for apps like chat applications, gaming, or collaborative platforms. **Firebase Realtime Database** or **AWS AppSync** provides real-time data synchronization across platforms.

- **File Storage and Media Management**: Cloud services like **Amazon S3**, **Google Cloud Storage**, and **Azure Blob Storage** provide scalable file storage solutions for managing large files such as images, videos, and documents.

Cloud Platforms to Use (AWS, Azure, Google Cloud)

When integrating cloud services into cross-platform applications, it's essential to choose the right cloud provider based on project needs, cost considerations, and available features. Here's an overview of the three major cloud platforms—**AWS**, **Azure**, and **Google Cloud**—and their offerings:

1. Amazon Web Services (AWS)

AWS is one of the most widely-used cloud platforms, offering a comprehensive suite of services for computing, storage, machine learning, and more.

- **Key Services for Cross-Platform Apps**:
    o **AWS Amplify**: A set of tools and services for building and deploying full-stack applications, including features like authentication, APIs, and storage.

    o **Amazon S3**: Object storage for large files such as images, videos, and backups. It's ideal for media management in cross-platform apps.

    o **Amazon Cognito**: A service for user authentication and authorization that allows you to add secure user sign-up, sign-in, and access control to apps.

    o **AWS Lambda**: Serverless computing that lets you run backend code without provisioning or managing servers. It's ideal for building scalable applications that respond to events or triggers.

- **When to Use AWS**:

    o Use AWS if you need a full suite of cloud services and require flexibility in choosing your infrastructure. AWS is highly customizable and is great for large-scale apps with complex backend needs.

2. Microsoft Azure

Azure is Microsoft's cloud platform, and it offers a variety of services, including support for cross-platform mobile apps, web applications, and enterprise-grade software.

- **Key Services for Cross-Platform Apps**:

    o **Azure Mobile Apps**: A platform for building mobile apps with integrated cloud services, including user authentication, push notifications, and offline sync.

o **Azure Functions**: Serverless computing for executing backend code in response to events without managing the server infrastructure.

o **Azure Blob Storage**: Scalable object storage for handling large amounts of unstructured data such as images and videos.

o **Azure Active Directory**: For managing user identities and authentication, especially useful for enterprise apps that require integration with Microsoft services.

- **When to Use Azure**:

  o Azure is a great choice for apps that are built in the Microsoft ecosystem or need to integrate with **Office 365**, **Dynamics 365**, or other Microsoft tools. It's also ideal for businesses already using **Windows Server** or **SQL Server** for on-premise infrastructure.

3. Google Cloud Platform (GCP)

Google Cloud offers a range of cloud services, from computing to storage, but it's especially well-known for its machine learning, big data, and AI services.

- **Key Services for Cross-Platform Apps**:
  - **Firebase**: A set of tools specifically designed for mobile and web app development, including features like real-time databases, authentication, analytics, and file storage. Firebase is easy to integrate into cross-platform mobile apps and simplifies backend management.
  - **Google Cloud Storage**: Scalable storage for large files such as media and backups, useful for apps that require extensive file handling.
  - **Google Cloud Functions**: Serverless computing for running backend code in response to events, ideal for cross-platform apps with simple backend requirements.

- o **Firebase Cloud Messaging (FCM)**: A service for sending push notifications to Android and iOS apps.

- **When to Use Google Cloud**:

  - o Google Cloud is great for startups and developers looking for a quick and easy solution for mobile app backends. If your app requires real-time data synchronization and fast deployment, **Firebase** is an excellent choice. Google Cloud also excels in data processing, machine learning, and AI-driven applications.

Real-World Example: Building an E-Commerce App with Integrated Cloud Services

Let's walk through a real-world example of how an e-commerce app is developed with integrated cloud services. The app needs to handle user authentication, product listings, payments, and real-time data syncing for inventory management, all while providing a consistent experience across both Android and iOS.

1. **App Requirements**:

   o **User Authentication**: Secure sign-up/sign-in process with multi-factor authentication.

   o **Product Listings**: Display products in real-time, with inventory data synced across all devices.

   o **Payment Processing**: Handle payments securely through integrated payment gateways.

   o **Real-Time Notifications**: Send notifications for order status updates and promotions.

2. **Choosing a Cloud Platform**:

   o The development team decides to use **Google Cloud** and **Firebase** due to the following reasons:

     ▪ **Firebase Authentication** provides a seamless sign-up/sign-in process across mobile platforms (Android and iOS).

164

- **Firebase Firestore** allows the team to manage real-time product listings, where changes to inventory or pricing are immediately reflected across devices.

- **Firebase Cloud Messaging** is used to send push notifications for order updates and promotional offers.

- **Firebase Storage** is used to store product images and media files.

3. **Setting Up Cloud Services**:

   o **Authentication**: Firebase Authentication is integrated into the mobile app, enabling users to sign up and log in with Google, Facebook, or email/password. Multi-factor authentication is enabled for added security.

   o **Real-Time Database**: Product data, including prices and inventory, is stored in **Firebase Firestore**. When a product is sold or restocked, Firestore syncs the changes in real-time across all devices using **Firestore's real-time capabilities**.

165

- o **Payment Gateway**: A third-party payment provider (such as **Stripe** or **PayPal**) is integrated via Firebase Cloud Functions to handle secure payment processing. This ensures that no sensitive information is stored directly in the app, enhancing security.

- o **Push Notifications**: Firebase Cloud Messaging (FCM) is used to send notifications to users about order status, discounts, and promotional messages. The app integrates FCM to push notifications on both iOS and Android devices.

4. **Deployment and Scalability**:

- o The app is deployed through **Firebase Hosting** to provide fast, scalable content delivery. Firebase handles the infrastructure management, so the development team can focus on building features.

- o The app is able to scale as demand grows by taking advantage of **Google Cloud Functions** and **Firestore** to handle increased load and traffic during sales or promotions.

5. **User Experience**:

   o The app provides a seamless, consistent experience across Android and iOS, with real-time updates on product availability, order status, and inventory changes. The cloud backend ensures that data is synchronized instantly between the client and server, regardless of the platform.

6. **Security**:

   o Sensitive data like payment information is securely handled through Firebase Cloud Functions, ensuring compliance with PCI DSS (Payment Card Industry Data Security Standard) requirements. Firebase Authentication and Firestore's built-in security rules ensure that user data is protected.

In this chapter, we explored how to integrate cloud services into cross-platform applications using popular cloud platforms like **AWS**, **Azure**, and **Google Cloud**. We also provided a real-world example of building an **e-commerce app** with integrated cloud services, demonstrating how Firebase can be used to handle authentication, real-time data synchronization, and notifications. In the next chapter, we will delve into best practices for testing and debugging cross-platform applications.

CHAPTER 14

TESTING AND DEBUGGING ACROSS PLATFORMS

Strategies for Testing Cross-Platform Applications

Testing cross-platform applications is essential to ensure that they function as expected on all platforms (Android, iOS, Windows, macOS, and web). Since cross-platform development involves writing a single codebase that runs across multiple platforms, testing must focus on verifying both the shared logic and the platform-specific behavior.

Here are some key strategies for testing cross-platform applications:

1. Platform-Specific Testing:

- Even though you're using a shared codebase, each platform has its unique set of behaviors and performance characteristics. It's essential to test your app on all target platforms (e.g., Android, iOS, web, desktop) to identify platform-specific issues, such as:

- o UI inconsistencies (different screen sizes, resolutions, or design guidelines).
- o Platform-specific APIs and permissions (e.g., location services on iOS vs. Android).
- o Device-specific performance (Android and iOS may perform differently on various devices).

Regularly testing on real devices, as opposed to just emulators or simulators, will help uncover issues that may not appear in the development environment.

2. Automated Cross-Platform Testing:

- **Automated testing** helps ensure that the app works consistently across platforms by running the same tests on different devices. Cross-platform testing tools like **Appium**, **XCUITest**, and **Espresso** allow for automated

UI and functional tests that can be run on both Android and iOS devices.

- o **Appium**: An open-source tool for automating mobile applications. It supports multiple platforms and programming languages, making it ideal for testing cross-platform mobile apps.

- o **XCUITest (iOS)** and **Espresso (Android)**: Native testing frameworks that allow you to automate functional tests, such as UI interactions and gestures, on real devices and simulators/emulators.

- o **Flutter**: For Flutter apps, you can use **Flutter Driver** to automate UI testing, ensuring that the app performs correctly across Android and iOS.

3. Continuous Integration (CI):

- Setting up a **Continuous Integration (CI)** pipeline helps automate the process of running tests on multiple platforms every time code is pushed to a repository. Using tools like **Jenkins**, **Travis CI**, or **CircleCI**, you can set

171

up workflows that test your app on multiple devices and platforms in parallel.

- CI pipelines can run tests on various environments (e.g., Android Emulator, iOS Simulator, or real devices) to catch issues before they make it into production.

4. Performance Testing:

- Testing performance across platforms is essential to ensure that your app runs smoothly on all devices. Tools like **Apache JMeter** or **Firebase Performance Monitoring** can be used to monitor network latency, CPU usage, memory consumption, and app startup times on different platforms.
- Regular profiling can help identify performance bottlenecks specific to certain platforms or devices and optimize the app's performance accordingly.

5. Manual Testing on Real Devices:

- While automated tests are great for covering many scenarios, some issues can only be caught through **manual testing**. Testing on physical devices is crucial for checking real-world performance, touch responsiveness, and UI rendering.

- Use device cloud platforms like **BrowserStack** or **Sauce Labs** to run manual tests on a variety of real devices without the need to own each device. These services provide access to a wide range of mobile and desktop devices for testing.

Unit Testing, Integration Testing, and Debugging Across Platforms

1. Unit Testing:

- Unit testing involves testing individual components or functions in isolation to ensure they work correctly. In cross-platform development, it's essential to write unit tests for core business logic and shared components.

- **Tools for Unit Testing**:

- o **JUnit** (for Java-based projects) or **NUnit** (for C#/.NET) for testing individual methods and functions.
- o **pytest** for Python-based unit testing.
- o **Flutter** provides built-in support for unit testing with **test** and **mockito** libraries for mocking dependencies.

- **Best Practices**:

  - o Isolate business logic from platform-specific code to ensure unit tests can run independently of the platform.
  - o Mock external services (e.g., API calls, databases) to focus only on the logic being tested.
  - o Write unit tests for platform-agnostic code that doesn't rely on UI components or device-specific APIs.

2. Integration Testing:

- Integration testing ensures that different parts of the application work together as expected. This includes

174

testing the interaction between the app's frontend and backend, as well as integration with external services like databases and APIs.

- **Tools for Integration Testing**:
  - o **Postman** or **RestAssured** for API testing.
  - o **Mockito** (for Java) and **NMock** (for C#) for mocking external services during integration tests.
  - o **Firebase Test Lab** for testing real-world app behavior on devices with integration to Firebase services.

- **Best Practices**:
  - o Perform end-to-end integration testing to ensure smooth communication between the app's different components.
  - o Test data synchronization between different platforms, ensuring consistency in user data, preferences, and settings.

  o Handle network latency and offline scenarios (e.g., when the app is offline and needs to sync data once reconnected).

3. Debugging Across Platforms:

- **Debugging** is the process of identifying and fixing errors in the code. Debugging cross-platform apps can be challenging due to platform-specific issues.

- **Common Tools**:

  o **Xcode Debugger** for iOS apps, which allows you to inspect variables, step through code, and view the call stack.

  o **Android Studio Debugger** for Android apps, with features like real-time debugging, inspecting network traffic, and viewing performance stats.

  o **Visual Studio Debugger** for Xamarin or C# apps that provides integrated debugging for both iOS and Android platforms.

o **Flutter DevTools** for debugging Flutter apps, including widget inspector, performance view, and logging tools.

- **Best Practices**:

  o Use logging extensively to track the flow of data and pinpoint where things go wrong. Both Android (Logcat) and iOS (Console) offer logging tools.

  o Utilize **remote debugging** to debug apps on real devices connected over Wi-Fi or USB.

  o Regularly use **profiling tools** to identify performance bottlenecks and memory leaks. Tools like **Xamarin Profiler** and **Android Profiler** can help isolate performance issues.

Real-World Example: Testing a Complex Cross-Platform Application with Multiple Users

Consider an e-commerce app developed using **React Native** that needs to support both Android and iOS users. The app has a large catalog of products, handles secure user logins, and integrates with a backend API for order processing and payment. Testing this app is a multi-faceted process that includes testing for functionality, performance, security, and cross-platform consistency.

1. **Unit Testing**:

   o The team writes unit tests for the core business logic, such as calculating product discounts, applying coupon codes, and updating the shopping cart. They use **Jest** for unit testing React Native components and business logic.

   o The business logic is isolated from platform-specific code, so unit tests run consistently on both Android and iOS.

178

2. Integration Testing:

o The team tests the integration of the front-end React Native app with the back-end API. They use **Postman** to test API endpoints for product listings, cart updates, and order processing.

o Real-time updates (such as stock availability) are tested using Firebase to ensure synchronization across all platforms.

o The app's payment gateway integration is tested with mock payment data to ensure that transactions are processed correctly.

3. Cross-Platform Manual Testing:

o The app undergoes manual testing on both Android and iOS to ensure UI consistency, smooth animations, and responsiveness. The team tests interactions like adding products to the cart, navigating between screens, and performing transactions.

- o Testing includes using **BrowserStack** for additional device testing across a range of Android and iOS devices.

4. **Performance Testing**:

- o The team uses **Firebase Performance Monitoring** to track app load times, API response times, and network latency. Performance bottlenecks are identified and optimized, such as lazy loading images and caching frequently accessed product data.

- o **JMeter** is used to simulate high traffic on the backend API to ensure that the app can handle a large number of concurrent users.

5. **Debugging**:

- o The team encounters an issue with slow image loading on older Android devices. Using **Android Studio Profiler**, they identify that unoptimized images are causing memory spikes. They optimize images and implement lazy loading to fix the issue.

- o **Xcode Debugger** is used to inspect iOS-specific performance issues, such as long startup times and slow network requests.

6. **Outcome**:

- o The testing process ensures that the app works seamlessly on both Android and iOS, handles user data securely, performs well under high traffic, and provides a smooth user experience. The app is ready for deployment, and the team can be confident in its performance and stability across platforms.

In this chapter, we explored the strategies and best practices for testing cross-platform applications, including unit testing, integration testing, and debugging. We also provided a real-world example of testing a complex e-commerce app with multiple users across Android and iOS. In the next chapter, we will discuss deployment strategies for cross-platform applications and how to ensure smooth releases across multiple platforms.

CHAPTER 15

DEPLOYMENT AND MAINTENANCE OF CROSS-PLATFORM APPS

Best Practices for Deploying Cross-Platform Applications

Once a cross-platform application has been tested and is ready for release, the deployment process begins. Ensuring a smooth deployment process across various platforms (Android, iOS, web, desktop) is essential to the success of the app. Below are some best practices for deploying cross-platform applications.

1. Automating Deployment

- **Use Automated Build Systems**: Automating the build process helps eliminate human error and ensures consistency in every deployment. For mobile apps, consider using tools like **Xcode** for iOS and **Android Studio** for Android to generate and test builds.

- **Automated Deployment**: Automating deployment is essential for maintaining consistent releases. Tools like **Fastlane** for iOS and Android apps can automate the release process, reducing the need for manual steps such as uploading to app stores or configuring deployment environments.

- **App Store Guidelines**: Ensure that your app adheres to platform-specific guidelines for submitting apps to the **Google Play Store** and **Apple App Store**. Both platforms have specific requirements for app size, icons, screenshots, and metadata. Review these requirements and ensure compliance to avoid delays during submission.

2. Versioning and Rollbacks

- **Version Control**: Maintain version control for the application to track and manage changes. Proper versioning ensures you can quickly fix bugs or introduce new features without disrupting existing users.

- **Rollbacks**: In case of issues with a new version, ensure that you have the ability to roll back to a previous stable version. Both **Google Play** and **Apple App Store** offer methods to roll back app updates in case of serious issues.

3. Environment Management

- **Multiple Environments**: It's essential to have separate environments for development, testing, staging, and production. Having different environments allows you to ensure that the app works as expected before going live and allows for a controlled release process.

- **Configuration Management**: Use configuration management tools to handle environment-specific configurations (e.g., API endpoints, credentials, third-party service keys) without hardcoding them into the app. This can be done using services like **Firebase Remote Config** or **AWS AppConfig**.

4. Cross-Platform Store Deployment

- **App Store (iOS)**: For iOS apps, deployment is done through **Xcode** and **TestFlight**. After building the app, upload the build to **App Store Connect**, configure the app's metadata, and submit it for review. If approved, it will be published on the App Store.

- **Google Play (Android)**: Android apps are deployed via **Google Play Console**. After building the app in **Android Studio**, it is uploaded to Google Play, where you can manage versions, track app performance, and monitor user feedback.

- **Web and Desktop**: For web apps, deploy them to platforms like **AWS**, **Google Cloud**, or **Microsoft Azure** using automated pipelines or manually via FTP. For desktop apps (Windows and macOS), you can package and distribute them using tools like **Electron** or **Xamarin**.

Continuous Integration and Delivery (CI/CD) Pipelines

Continuous Integration (CI) and **Continuous Delivery (CD)** are crucial practices in modern app development. They automate the processes of integrating code changes and delivering them to users, ensuring quicker and more reliable deployments.

1. Continuous Integration (CI)

- **Automated Builds**: CI tools automatically trigger builds whenever new code is pushed to the repository. This ensures that the latest code changes are tested and compiled into an app build. Popular CI tools include **Jenkins, GitLab CI, Travis CI**, and **CircleCI**.

- **Unit and Integration Testing**: After each build, automated tests (unit tests, integration tests) are executed to ensure that no new bugs have been introduced. This allows developers to catch issues early and reduce manual testing.

- **Code Quality Checks**: CI systems can automatically check for code quality by running static analysis tools such as **SonarQube** or **ESLint**, which help maintain consistent code standards.

2. Continuous Delivery (CD)

- **Automated Deployment**: Once the code passes CI tests, it is automatically deployed to different environments such as staging or production. This reduces the risk of manual errors and speeds up the release process. Tools like **Fastlane** can automate deployments to both **Google Play** and **App Store**.

- **Rolling Updates**: In the case of mobile applications, it's important to ensure that updates don't disrupt the user experience. Rolling updates allow developers to push updates incrementally, ensuring smooth updates for users. For example, **Google Play** supports staged rollouts, where only a percentage of users receive the update at first.

- **Canary Releases**: Canary releases allow new versions of the app to be deployed to a small subset of users to monitor performance before a full rollout. This is helpful in identifying issues in real-world conditions.

3. CI/CD Tools and Platforms

- **Jenkins**: An open-source CI/CD tool widely used for automating the building, testing, and deploying of apps.
- **GitLab CI**: An integrated CI/CD solution that is built into GitLab and provides end-to-end automation for code integration and deployment.
- **Travis CI**: A CI/CD service that integrates directly with GitHub repositories, providing an easy-to-use platform for building and deploying apps.
- **CircleCI**: A powerful CI/CD tool for automating deployments that integrates with GitHub and Bitbucket repositories.
- **Fastlane**: Automates the process of building, testing, and releasing mobile applications. Fastlane integrates well with both iOS and Android.

Real-World Example: A Step-by-Step Guide to Deploying a Cross-Platform App to the Cloud

Let's walk through the process of deploying a **cross-platform mobile app** (built with **React Native**) to the cloud, with continuous integration and delivery set up to streamline the process.

1. **App Overview**:
   - The app is a **task management application** that syncs tasks across devices (Android and iOS) using a cloud database (Firebase). It also uses cloud storage (Google Cloud Storage) for storing images and attachments.

2. **Setting Up CI/CD**:
   - **GitHub Repository**: The project code is stored in a **GitHub** repository. All code changes trigger the CI/CD pipeline.
   - **Continuous Integration**:

- **GitHub Actions** is used to automate the build process. Whenever code is pushed to the repository, GitHub Actions triggers the build and tests the app.

- The CI pipeline includes steps for:

  - Installing dependencies using **npm**.

  - Running unit and integration tests.

  - Building the app for both Android and iOS using **React Native**.

o **Continuous Delivery**:

  - Once the build passes all tests, the app is automatically uploaded to **Firebase** for staging (pre-production environment).

  - After testing in staging, the app is deployed to production through **Fastlane**, which automates the process of

191

releasing the app to the **Google Play Store** and **Apple App Store**.

3. **Cloud Integration**:

   o The app integrates with **Firebase** for real-time data syncing and **Google Cloud Storage** for managing media uploads.

   o Firebase authentication is set up to allow users to sign in with Google, Facebook, or email/password.

   o **Firebase Firestore** is used to store user tasks, and real-time synchronization ensures that changes are reflected immediately across all devices.

4. **Testing**:

   o The development team uses **Firebase Test Lab** to run automated UI tests on real devices across multiple platforms. These tests check for consistency in UI rendering, performance, and functionality across Android and iOS.

   o **TestFlight** is used for distributing the app to beta testers on iOS. Android users receive updates through the **Google Play Store** via staged rollouts.

5. **Deployment**:

   o   After successful testing, the app is submitted for review to both the **Google Play Store** and **Apple App Store**.

   o   The CI/CD pipeline ensures that the latest build is automatically pushed to both stores as soon as it's ready.

6. **Monitoring and Maintenance**:

   o   **Google Analytics** and **Firebase Crashlytics** are used to monitor the app's performance and capture errors in real time.

   o   Regular updates are pushed to fix bugs, add new features, and improve performance. The CI/CD pipeline ensures that updates are released efficiently, keeping the app fresh and bug-free.

In this chapter, we discussed best practices for deploying and maintaining cross-platform apps, including automating the deployment process, using CI/CD pipelines, and ensuring cloud integration. We also walked through a real-world example of deploying a React Native app with cloud services integrated, showing how CI/CD, cloud storage, and Firebase authentication streamline deployment and maintenance. In the next chapter, we will explore app store optimization (ASO) strategies to help get your app noticed by users.

CHAPTER 16

THE FUTURE OF CROSS-PLATFORM DEVELOPMENT

Emerging Trends in Cross-Platform Development

As technology continues to evolve, cross-platform development is also advancing, making it easier to build applications that work seamlessly across multiple devices and platforms. In this chapter, we'll explore some of the emerging trends in cross-platform development and how they are shaping the future of app development. These trends include the rise of **AI**, **machine learning**, and **the Internet of Things (IoT)**, and how they are transforming how cross-platform applications are built and used.

1. AI and Machine Learning Integration

- **Automating User Experience**: Artificial intelligence and machine learning are increasingly being integrated into cross-platform applications to create personalized experiences. Apps can now use **AI algorithms** to analyze user behavior, predict needs, and adapt the interface in real-time. This is becoming essential for improving user retention and engagement.

- **Natural Language Processing (NLP)**: AI-powered NLP allows cross-platform apps to offer advanced voice commands, chatbots, and virtual assistants. Platforms like **Google's DialogFlow**, **Apple's SiriKit**, and **Amazon's Alexa** are being integrated into apps to provide seamless voice-controlled experiences.

- **Image and Video Recognition**: With AI models like **Google Vision** and **TensorFlow**, cross-platform apps can now process and recognize images and video content, making it possible to build apps that use **augmented reality (AR)** or **computer vision** for a wide range of applications, from retail and entertainment to security.

- **Predictive Analytics**: Machine learning algorithms are being used to analyze user data, allowing apps to predict user behavior, optimize performance, and provide intelligent recommendations. For example, **Spotify** uses machine learning to suggest music based on listening history.

2. IoT Integration in Cross-Platform Apps

- **The Rise of Connected Devices**: The Internet of Things (IoT) refers to the growing network of devices that connect to the internet and can communicate with each other. IoT is becoming an essential part of cross-platform development, as many apps are now expected to interact with a wide range of smart devices, including home automation systems, wearables, and industrial sensors.

- **Smart Homes and Wearables**: Cross-platform apps are integrating IoT features to manage smart home devices like thermostats, security cameras, and lighting systems. Additionally, wearable devices such as smartwatches and fitness trackers are generating massive amounts of data that cross-platform apps can leverage for health, fitness, and lifestyle applications.

197

- **Real-Time Data**: IoT apps often require real-time data syncing between devices. Cross-platform frameworks like **Flutter**, **React Native**, and **Xamarin** allow apps to communicate with cloud services and IoT devices seamlessly, providing users with real-time updates and control over connected devices.

- **Industry Applications**: IoT is transforming industries like healthcare, logistics, agriculture, and manufacturing. Cross-platform apps are being developed to monitor and control devices in these sectors, improving efficiency, safety, and productivity.

3. AR and VR Integration

- **Augmented Reality (AR)** and **Virtual Reality (VR)** are becoming more integrated into cross-platform applications. With tools like **ARCore** (for Android) and **ARKit** (for iOS), developers are building immersive AR experiences that allow users to interact with their environment in real-time.

- Cross-platform frameworks like **Unity** and **Flutter** support AR and VR integration, enabling developers to create apps that deliver immersive experiences across devices.

4. Low-Code and No-Code Development

- **Low-code** and **no-code** development platforms are gaining popularity, especially for non-technical users who want to create cross-platform applications. These platforms enable developers to build apps with minimal coding by using visual interfaces and pre-built components.
- This trend allows businesses to create custom applications more quickly and efficiently, reducing the development cycle and making app creation more accessible to a wider audience.

5. Cloud-Native Cross-Platform Apps

- The shift toward cloud-native architectures is having a significant impact on cross-platform development. By leveraging cloud services, developers can build apps that are more scalable, flexible, and resilient. Cross-platform apps can rely on cloud-based backend services for storage, processing, and real-time data syncing.

- Tools like **AWS Amplify**, **Google Firebase**, and **Microsoft Azure** are simplifying the process of integrating cloud services into cross-platform apps, making it easier to develop and deploy applications that scale across platforms.

How AI, Machine Learning, and IoT Are Shaping the Future of Cross-Platform Apps

1. AI-Powered Personalization

- Machine learning algorithms will enable cross-platform apps to adapt in real-time to user preferences and behavior, creating a more personalized experience.

Whether it's recommending products, services, or content, AI will play a central role in improving user engagement and satisfaction.

- For example, in an e-commerce app, AI can help personalize the shopping experience by recommending products based on past purchases, browsing behavior, and even predicting future needs.

2. Real-Time IoT Data Sync

- IoT integration will enable real-time data synchronization across devices. Cross-platform apps that use IoT will need to provide users with live data updates from connected devices. This will be especially useful in applications like home automation, healthcare monitoring, and vehicle tracking.

- With cloud services enabling the storage and processing of IoT data, cross-platform apps will be able to handle large volumes of real-time data, providing users with actionable insights and control over their devices.

3. AI and IoT for Smart Cities and Industries

- Smart city applications and industrial IoT will benefit greatly from AI and cross-platform development. From traffic management to smart grids, cross-platform apps will play a central role in controlling and monitoring IoT devices deployed throughout urban areas and industries.

- In manufacturing, for example, IoT-enabled cross-platform apps can monitor machine health in real-time, predict failures, and automate maintenance schedules using AI.

4. Enhanced AR/VR Experiences

- With AR and VR gaining popularity, especially in gaming, retail, and training applications, cross-platform apps will be designed to deliver immersive experiences on both mobile and desktop devices. AR apps will provide users with virtual try-ons, virtual home tours, and interactive learning, all accessible across platforms.

Real-World Example: A Forward-Looking Company Integrating IoT Features into Its Cross-Platform App

Example: SmartHome Solutions

Company Overview: SmartHome Solutions is a company that provides smart home automation products, including smart thermostats, security cameras, lighting systems, and voice-activated assistants. They have developed a cross-platform app that allows users to control and monitor their smart home devices from their smartphones, tablets, and desktops.

Challenges:

- The app needs to work across multiple platforms (iOS, Android, web, and desktop).
- The app must interact with a wide range of IoT devices, such as thermostats, cameras, and lighting systems, ensuring real-time updates.

- The app needs to provide users with intelligent features, such as predictive automation, based on user behavior and preferences.

Solution:

SmartHome Solutions chooses to build their app using **React Native** for mobile and **Electron** for desktop, ensuring that the app works seamlessly across platforms. The app integrates **IoT sensors** and devices into the system to provide real-time data, which is managed through **Google Firebase** and **AWS IoT Core**. The app also uses **AI** to learn user behavior, like adjusting the thermostat based on preferred temperatures at specific times of day.

1. **Cross-Platform Development**:
   - **React Native** is used to build the mobile app, enabling it to work on both **Android** and **iOS**. **Electron** is used to create the desktop version of

the app, ensuring consistency across mobile and desktop platforms.

o The app communicates with IoT devices via **AWS IoT Core**, which handles data from the devices in real-time and synchronizes it across all platforms.

2. **Real-Time IoT Data Sync**:

o IoT sensors placed in the home provide real-time data, such as temperature readings, motion detection, and camera feeds. This data is sent to the cloud, where it's processed and made available to the app.

o The app uses **Firebase Realtime Database** for real-time syncing between devices. If a user adjusts the thermostat on their phone, the change is reflected on their tablet and desktop immediately.

3. **AI and Machine Learning**:

o The app uses **machine learning** to predict the user's behavior. For example, the thermostat adjusts automatically based on user behavior patterns. If the user typically lowers the temperature at night, the app learns this pattern and adjusts the temperature autonomously.

o The AI also powers the **voice-activated assistant**, which allows users to control devices with simple voice commands like "Turn off the lights" or "Set the thermostat to 72 degrees."

4. **Deployment and Scalability**:

o The app is deployed to the **Google Play Store**, **Apple App Store**, and distributed to users via **Electron** on desktops. The cloud backend scales with demand, ensuring the app remains responsive even with a growing number of users and IoT devices.

5. **Outcome**:

o The SmartHome Solutions app provides a seamless, intelligent home automation experience for users across platforms. It can interact with a wide range of IoT devices, provide real-time control and feedback, and make the home environment more efficient using AI-powered automation.

In this chapter, we've explored the emerging trends in cross-platform development, including how **AI**, **machine learning**, and **IoT** are shaping the future of app development. We also provided a real-world example of how a forward-looking company integrated IoT features into its cross-platform app, demonstrating how cloud services, real-time data synchronization, and AI can work together to create intelligent and scalable apps. In the next chapter, we will discuss the importance of app store optimization (ASO) and strategies for improving app visibility in the marketplace.

CHAPTER 18

FINAL THOUGHTS AND BUILDING YOUR CROSS-PLATFORM FUTURE

Recap of Key Concepts and Takeaways

As we've explored throughout this book, the world of cross-platform development is rapidly evolving, offering developers the tools and frameworks they need to build applications that work seamlessly across multiple devices and platforms. Let's take a moment to recap the key concepts and takeaways from our journey:

1. Cross-Platform Development Frameworks:

- We covered the most popular frameworks such as **React Native, Xamarin, Flutter, Kivy**, and **BeeWare**. Each of these has its unique strengths, from **React Native's** ability to build performant apps with JavaScript to **Xamarin's** integration with the **.NET ecosystem** for building native apps across Android and iOS.

- **Flutter** stood out with its rich UI components and performance, making it an excellent choice for building visually appealing apps across mobile, web, and desktop platforms.

2. Cloud Integration and Backend Services:

- Cloud services play a crucial role in cross-platform development, enabling real-time data synchronization, file storage, and authentication. **AWS, Google Cloud,** and **Microsoft Azure** offer various services tailored to cross-platform apps.

- We explored how **Firebase** and **AWS Amplify** simplify the process of integrating backend services like authentication, databases, and push notifications, allowing you to focus on building your app's front-end.

3. Testing and Debugging Across Platforms:

- A comprehensive testing strategy is essential for cross-platform apps, ensuring that your application works across all devices and operating systems. We discussed the importance of **unit testing**, **integration testing**, and **manual testing on real devices**.

- Debugging across platforms can be challenging, but tools like **Xcode Debugger**, **Android Studio**, and **Visual Studio Debugger** make it easier to pinpoint and resolve issues, ensuring a smoother user experience.

4. Continuous Integration and Deployment:

- **CI/CD pipelines** are vital for automating the build, test, and deployment processes, ensuring that new changes are delivered quickly and reliably. Tools like **Jenkins**, **GitLab CI**, and **Fastlane** help streamline this process.

- We also discussed **app store deployment** and the importance of following platform-specific guidelines for submitting your app to the **Google Play Store** and **Apple App Store**.

5. The Future of Cross-Platform Development:

- The future of cross-platform development is intertwined with emerging technologies like **AI**, **machine learning**, and **IoT**. We've seen how these technologies are revolutionizing the way apps are developed, offering personalized experiences, real-time data syncing, and integration with connected devices.

- The integration of **AR**, **VR**, and **cloud-native development** will continue to expand the capabilities of cross-platform apps, creating even more immersive and scalable applications.

Encouragement to Start a Real-World Cross-Platform Project

Now that we've explored the landscape of cross-platform development, the next step is to **start building** your own cross-platform application. Whether you're working on your first app or looking to expand your skills, there's no better time than now to dive into a real-world project.

Here are a few tips to get started:

1. **Pick a Simple Idea**:
   - Start with a simple app idea that interests you. It could be something like a **task manager**, a **weather app**, or even a **budget tracker**. The key is to focus on building something manageable that incorporates essential features like authentication, data storage, and a clean user interface.

2. **Choose the Right Tools**:
   - Based on your app idea, choose a framework that fits your needs. For example, if you're focused on a sleek UI, **Flutter** may be your best choice. If you're already familiar with **C#**, then **Xamarin** will be a natural fit. Start with something that aligns with your skills and interests, but don't

hesitate to explore other frameworks down the line.

3. **Learn by Building**:

   o The best way to learn is by doing. As you build your app, you'll encounter real-world problems and challenges, which will help you learn the nuances of cross-platform development. Don't worry about making mistakes—each one is an opportunity to grow and improve.

4. **Use Cloud Services and Backend Integration**:

   o Incorporate cloud services like **Firebase** or **AWS** into your app to handle backend operations like user authentication, data storage, and real-time synchronization. This will give your app scalability and allow you to focus on the front-end user experience.

5. **Test and Iterate**:

   o Testing is critical to the development process. Regularly test your app on multiple platforms to ensure it works as expected. Make use of automated testing tools like **Appium** or **XCUITest** for mobile apps, and **Jest** for unit testing in **React Native**.

6. **Deploy and Get Feedback**:

   o Once your app is ready, deploy it to app stores or share it with friends and family to get feedback. If it's a web app, deploy it to cloud services like **Firebase Hosting** or **AWS Amplify**. Use feedback to improve the app, fix bugs, and introduce new features.

Remember, building a cross-platform app is a journey, and it's important to embrace the learning process. The more projects you work on, the more proficient you'll become in creating powerful, scalable apps that reach a wider audience.

Real-World Example: A Developer's Journey from Learning Cross-Platform Tools to Creating Their First App

Developer's Journey:

Let's follow the journey of **Alex**, a developer who decided to venture into cross-platform development after working on a few native Android apps. Alex had a background in Java, but they were intrigued by the idea of building apps that could run on both **Android** and **iOS** without writing separate code for each platform.

Phase 1: Learning Cross-Platform Tools

Alex started by researching different cross-platform tools and eventually chose **Flutter** because of its ease of use, vibrant community, and strong documentation. They followed tutorials and took online courses to understand how to build mobile apps using **Dart** and **Flutter**.

215

During this phase, Alex learned how to build user interfaces, integrate cloud services (using **Firebase**), and handle platform-specific APIs. They built simple apps like a **to-do list** and a **weather app** to practice what they had learned.

Phase 2: Building the First Real-World App

Once Alex was comfortable with Flutter, they decided to tackle a more challenging project: building a **recipe app** that allows users to search for, save, and share recipes. The app needed to support both **Android** and **iOS**, so Alex focused on making sure the user interface was clean and responsive on both platforms.

- **Backend**: Alex integrated **Firebase Authentication** to allow users to sign in with Google accounts and **Firestore** for saving user preferences and recipes.
- **Cloud Integration**: They used **Firebase Storage** to allow users to upload images of their recipes, while **Firebase**

Realtime Database synced data between users' devices in real time.

Phase 3: Testing and Deployment

Alex used **Flutter's testing framework** to write unit tests for the app's core features, such as searching for recipes and saving favorites. After thoroughly testing the app on both Android and iOS simulators, they deployed it to **Google Play Store** and **Apple App Store** for beta testing.

During the testing phase, Alex received valuable feedback from users about performance issues and suggested improvements. They made some optimizations, fixed bugs, and launched the app to a wider audience.

Phase 4: Iterating and Scaling

After the initial launch, Alex continued to improve the app by adding new features, such as recipe sharing and social media integration. They also started using **Google Analytics** and **Firebase Crashlytics** to monitor app performance and fix issues as they arose.

Alex's first app was a success, and this experience gave them the confidence to build more complex cross-platform apps in the future.

In this chapter, we've recapped the essential concepts of cross-platform development, from frameworks and cloud integration to testing and deployment. We also encouraged you to start your own cross-platform project and provided a real-world example of a developer's journey from learning cross-platform tools to creating their first app. By following in these footsteps, you can begin your own journey and create apps that work across multiple platforms, reach a global audience, and make an impact. The future of cross-platform development is bright, and now is the perfect time to build your app.

www.ingramcontent.com/pod-product-compliance
Lightning Source LLC
LaVergne TN
LVHW051325050326
832903LV00031B/3370